Steady as a Rock:
The Maynard Surber Story

by Pat Lawrence

The book was commissioned by Connie and John Surber to honor and celebrate the life and legacy of a very special man. It is told in Maynard's own words, transcribed from audiotapes he made and gathered through interviews with him, his sons James and John and his daughter-in-law, Connie. It is dedicated to the next generations of Surbers, the young men and women who share a heritage rooted in the land and who will carry on the resolute, inquiring spirit of Maynard Surber.

Staff Sergeant Maynard Surber

CHAPTER 1

The Family and the Farm

I'm Maynard Surber. I was born in the back room of this house, raised on the land that seven generations of my family have lived on since 1797. Not too many people have lived in the same place for 215 years, but we have. My father, Earl Surber, built this house in 1915 for about $1500 from a blueprint he got from California. He made the concrete blocks himself, two at a time and every stick of wood was cut from our farm. Except for a little wear and tear, a lot of photos on the walls, and a little extra space we added when the boys got too big to sleep in our room, it doesn't look much different than when I arrived April 14th in 1920.

Our family originally came over from the Shenandoah Valley, one of seventeen families that settled in the country outside of Hillsboro, Ohio, just at the turn of the century. We're the last farm that has one of the original family names. In Switzerland, there's a Surb River and that's where our people came from.

The first one to come over was Henry. He was just 17 or 18 when he arrived, but he married and had two sons. One of them, Jacob, became an Indian scout. After the Revolutionary War, Jacob kept scouting, only he scouted for the surveyors that were mapping out the country. He's the one who encouraged the seventeen families to come with him to the new Ohio territory, which didn't become a state until 1803. They picked out the land they wanted along Smokey Row Creek and White Oak Creek and paid a dollar an acre for the privilege of squatting on it. Turned out to be a good investment for everyone. They say Smokey Row Creek was named by the Indians for the smoke that floated down from the settlers' log cabins but I don't believe that.

The settlers initially built a church at either end of the land, but when they finally got the forests cleared, they met in the middle and named their community Union. My great-grandfather John Perry Surber was born on the Surber homestead in 1832. He was a religious man; he helped establish the Union church and was an elder there for fifty-six years. His wife, Sara, died in an epidemic, probably influenza, along with their three sons in 1860. A year later, he married Sara's sister, Jennie, and they had five children, four that lived. Great-grandpa wanted to make a preacher out of his oldest son, my great-uncle Claude, and sent him to Butler University. But Claude just wasn't preacher material. He ended up at Johns Hopkins and became a doctor. Besides doctoring, he became a millionaire on the stock market. Even after he took a loss in the crash, Claude still had quite a lot. Several years after his wife died, great-uncle Claude developed cancer. Finally, he just laid down on his couch, gave himself a shot, closed his eyes and died there at home.

It was the youngest son, Lewis, who was the one interested in the farming operation. He built his house on the farm in 1888 and added the farm buildings in 1903.

By his later years, John Perry had divided most of his estate between his two daughters and Claude and Lewis. He decided to sell 152 acres including most of the original 100 acre tract and homestead. Claude had his own career and Lewis figured he had all the land he needed. Great-grandpa was selling out but the sons weren't interested in buying. So, great-grandpa sold his property to a German family, the Toedters. I was told they came here from Minnesota; that they had been threatened because of bad feelings to Germans, not unusual after WWI. They packed their bags, but didn't know where to go. According to the story, they had a map of the United States and just picked a place at random. The only farm available in the area was the nearly 160 acres of our original settlement. Our family should'a bought it back then, I reckon, but we didn't. There's still a lot of bad feeling about that to this day.

In 1924, during a trip from Lebanon to Muncie, Indiana, John Perry and two of his grandsons were involved in an accident north of Winchester, Indiana and he was fatally injured. I remember his funeral. They picked me up and let me look into the casket.

My grandfather Lewis was active in the church, but not as much as his father. Lewis was a great innovator himself. He appreciated new ideas and good technology and implemented the latest farming methods and soil erosion prevention. He was constantly investigating and trying new practices and methodology that would improve the land and crops. He was a hard worker, too. He set trees, tilled the land and built fences.

As a youth, Lewis was what was known as a "dandy". He always drove a fine horse and buggy, dressed well and was very socially outgoing. He played trumpet in the community band which would perform at all occasions and celebrations. It was at one of these celebrations that he met Anna Pegan who would later become his wife. Her father, a Civil War veteran, had been captured and held for some time in a confederate prison. After the war he returned home physically limited to fairly light work but he raised his family on a disability pension of $12 per month. Grandma Anna was known as the prettiest girl in the area in spite of a decided limp from a broken leg at the age of twelve.

Grandpa Lew always had the first and best of anything. His first automobile was a Maxwell in about 1910. There were hundreds of different car companies back then, some only made half a dozen cars. There was even an auto maker in Greenfield! Later, Grandpa had a Willys-Knight, an automobile manufactured between 1914 and 1933 by the Willys-Overland Company of Toledo, Ohio. They produced about 50,000 cars a year in the 20's. It was a good car; he kept it thirteen years and it had 13,000 miles on it. Gas was ten cents a gallon back then. We had a 50 gallon tank on the property and it lasted about a year. That car ran for a year for $5. 'Course, we only went to Hillsboro once a month, when the weather was good. We never took the car.

In 1926, Grandpa had the first radio in the community. I remember the Dempsey-Tunney heavyweight fight in 1927 when all the men of the community gathered in the summer kitchen to hear it on the radio. There were at least 25 in attendance. Grandpa was always a hunter and during the season, friends from far away came to hunt quail and rabbits.

This was not always a joy to Grandma, since she had to cook for them.

For a farmer in the early 1900's, he traveled quite a bit- he had attended the World's Fair at St. Louis in 1903. He was a member of many of the local organizations and was a Mason until his death.

He was diagnosed with cancer when he was 62. The doctor had told him he was dying and he knew his time was almost over. One day near the end, Grandpa Lewis called all of us over to his house and told Mom and Dad they needed to go clear out the safe deposit box. Back then, there was taxes to be paid on the contents of safe deposit boxes and no one wanted that so Dad and Mom took Cedric and hotfooted it to the bank and left me with Grandpa. While they were gone and we were alone, grandpa asked me to make him a promise. He wanted my word that I would stay on the farm, make it my life. He said it was the most important thing I could do for him. There wasn't much discussion; there was really just one answer. I made the promise. He died on May 05, 1930.

Back then, big families were typical but not for us; Dad was an only child. He was born in the house my brother Cedric lives in now. He and my mother lived with my grandparents while Dad worked with a master carpenter and his assistant to built their house. They had let the wood they'd cut for the house sit for two years before construction started. The master carpenter, Fred Liebert, made $1.50 a day and his assistant made 75 cents, working from dawn to dusk.

Cedric came along three years after me but we were always close. The farm was 260 acres and we had a little of everything - chickens, cattle, hogs. We bought very little at the grocery store, just sugar, coffee and coal oil for the lamps. People were still driving buggies when I was born. Women drove the buggies but they weren't supposed to drive the cars. They weren't emancipated yet.

Our family got electricity in 1932, but before that we made our own electricity with a big battery that had a gas engine. We could only use one 25-watt bulb at a time. Each battery was as big as a trash can and we kept half a dozen of them. They sat on wood 2x8's, with the motor right beside them to hook them up.

In 1932, we got together and paid for the power lines to be put in. Back then, each town had their own electric plant. They charged us $3.75 a month for the electricity. First thing we bought was a toaster; 3-4 years later, we got a refrigerator.

My father, Earl, was a different man than his father. Dad wasn't much for working, though he handled the banking and finances for his father and grandfather. He liked to go into town to "handle business", but I think that business was mostly drinking coffee, or something stronger, and swapping stories with his friends. He was a deacon in the church for many years. He did carry forth his father's plans in soil and game management and he was on the board of the first Soil and Water Conservation District in the County. He liked to hunt and trap and was the first Surber to attend college at Ohio State in Agriculture, taking what was called then, "A Short Course in General Farming".

He met my mother, Ganelle Roberts, when she would visit her aunt Ollie Winkle at the Winkle homestead, two farms north of ours. Earl and Ganelle lived in the house he built for the rest of their lives. They never traveled far from home, except for the family's World's Fair trip in 1933 even though we always had a car.

We were political people. We never missed voting; Mom voted, too. The Surbers were Democrats and the in-laws were Republicans, so there was an argument over politics every time we got together, which was about every Sunday. Everybody should vote. I can't understand people who won't vote. I can't imagine what would happen to us if we lost the right to vote.

I was five when I started school. I reckon they wanted to get me out of the house. I was supposed to start first grade at the one-room Union School house, but I was the only first-grader enrolled, so the teachers asked my parents if they could put me in second grade instead. I was always the brat in the class and being two years younger than the rest of the class kept me apart from the other students. They didn't want me at any class parties. Maybe that's why I read right from the beginning. I read anything I could get a hold of. I never cared much for fiction-I liked history and geography. Still, I was usually ahead of the rest of the class because of all that reading.

On the first day of school, I didn't know you were supposed to come home right after so I didn't go straight home. We all walked to school then, naturally. Didn't know everybody was out looking for me. I was chastised for that with a switch on the butt! Never did that a second time! Boys anywhere get in trouble, but we had a boys Sunday school class. If any of us got out of hand, whatever older man was there would reach over and pull our hair. Everybody was concerned about discipline. In those days, if you needed it, they gave it to you; if grandpa thought I needed a switch, I got it!

We never went anywhere, we just played with the local kids for entertainment, and Cedric and I participated in 4H when we were growing up, but in 1932, the family went to the World's Fair in Chicago. I was about 12 and Cedric was about 9. Clinton County was taking a group and didn't have enough people signed up. We went by train- it took all day to get there - and stayed at the Stockyards Hotel. We dressed up to go. Dad wore a suit, mom wore a hat. It was promoted as an exposition of Science, Industry and Art and it was all that.

The automobile industry had the largest contingent at the Fair. Each of the Big Three had their own pavilion along with Nash, Cord, Packard, Pierce-Arrow and some original inventors displaying their dream cars. The Golden Packard was trimmed in real gold and Dusenberg displayed their Twenty Grand model- that's what it sold for! That would have bought you forty new Plymouth coupes with change to spare!

There were villages of all the different people set up at The World section of the fair- China, India, Japan, Egypt, Morocco, Ukraine- a lot of different countries were represented. There was a Mayan Temple and an Indian Village with tepees and totem poles. And there was all the newest technology, including a television demonstration. A little girl would stand in front of something like a camera and the image was projected about 40 feet away. We watched them make tires, and that really impressed me, and saw Sally Rand dance with her feathers. You couldn't see it all in just 3-4 days, but we were great gawkers. We didn't ride the skyway. I think the old folks were scared. It was 600 feet up, supported by towers. Just getting into a taxi in the big city was scary enough for us.

That was the only time we ever left home. I was 18 before I crossed the Ohio state line again.

I got out of Mowrystown High School at 15. That's when Dad told Cedric and I that we were going to be running the farm from then on. He pretty much quit working on the farm after that. That winter, I took the short course for farmers at Ohio State University. It lasted 4-5 months. I fell in love there - with Ayrshire cattle. I shared a room with one bed with another fellow taking the course-we'd never even met before- and learned about dairying and agriculture.

My brother was just 12, but we decided we wanted to go into business together with dairy cattle. Dad didn't believe in milking, he wanted to raise beef cattle, but he bought the cows for us and paid about $150 apiece for them. We started with 3-4 heifers; by the time the war began we had a reasonable-sized herd of 20-40 which grew to 150 after the war. I loved Ayrshire cattle - their red and white color and their fancy horns; they were different and they just appealed to me. It was the beginning of a lifetime association.

From when I was 16 until 1986, we were in the Ayrshire business. We were the first to bring Ayrshires into this county. We milked with a stool and a bucket the first 3-4 years, but eventually we bought milkers. I didn't buy the best equipment. You couldn't be a success back then if you spent your money on the best. The more manual labor we did, the more money we made. Like any business, when you give all your effort to something, it pays off.

We kept the milk in gallon crocks but we only sold cream. We used a separator, adding water to the milk and letting gravity do the work. The cream rose to the top and there was a spigot to drain off the water. We used some of the milk to make cottage cheese and fed the leftover milk to the pigs. The cottage cheese was much better than what comes from the store now. After Carnation opened their condensed milk plant in Hillsboro, we began selling them milk. A lot of other folks in the area did, too. It was quite a business. Carnation paid 75 cents per hundred pounds of milk; we sold $2800 worth of milk one year. My brother and I split the profit and paid our expenses out of it. Carnation eventually closed their Hillsboro plant on Water Street and moved the operation to Maysville, Kentucky.

When we weren't in school or working, I always liked to read- and sing. I always sang in church. Except during the war, I bet I didn't miss ten Sundays in my life from church, not that I was that religious, but I had to lead the singing. I sang all over, in quartets, by myself, with just about anyone. I was in the quartet that Mary Muntz organized. Mary gave away everything she made to kids. She was a teacher who taught in all the Highland County schools, and she'd take us to contests and amateur nights. In high school, our quartet would win just about every time. They had amateur nights at the Colony Theater almost every week; we'd win there too. We sang for senior citizens and organizations all over. My great-uncle Claude used to give me fifty-cent pieces when I'd sing. I'd never seen money before and that was BIG money!

I kept singing- religious music, comedy, popular music. There were ladies in all the different areas I knew that would play for me so I didn't have to bring an accompanist. I sang at hundreds of funerals, even for people I didn't know. Around 1936, I remember we sang at a businessmen's meeting where they had black waiters serving the tables. One of the song's had lyrics about "the coon in the woodpile". We didn't know any better then. But, I think about it now, what did those waiters think of us? Things have changed a lot in the last fifty years, and rightfully so.

In the 30's, the depression was on and boys didn't have money. My friend Carrol Bennington and I would spend the week trying to get a quarter. We'd each buy a gallon of gas, then we'd go to the smokery and buy a cigar, two for a nickel. After that, we'd just stand around and watch the girls go by.

There weren't many ways for girls to meet eligible young men so mothers would bring their daughters downtown to show them off. From 6-10 in the evening, there was such a crowd in downtown Hillsboro, you could barely walk. One woman in particular always came with her two good-lookin' daughters. Another friend of ours liked one of the daughters especially. He told us, "I'm gonna marry that one." And he did.

I was just there for the entertainment. Growing up, one of the girls in my class was America Isabelle Donohoo. We even sang together. The first time we performed, we were about six. We hated each other, of course, but we got over that. The Donohoo farm, and Isabelle's family, had been there since 1840. We didn't have what people call a romantic relationship, but I think everyone had figured we'd get married since we were born.

CHAPTER 2

Called to War

Although the nation had begun preparing for war, interest in the war built rapidly after Pearl Harbor. After December 7th , things changed dramatically and fast. Within a couple weeks, I was notified by my draft board to report. I'd been thinking about it anyway I was already registered for the draft but I hadn't anticipated being called at such an early time. One boy had to stay on the farm and that was going to be Cedric. After just six weeks of waiting, by Feb 22, 42, I was called into the service. My service wasn't any more important than anyone else's, but it was mine.

On the morning of February 22, 1942, Isabelle took me up to Hillsboro to the Armory and there 20 some of us were met by the draft board members. After all the paperwork was completed, they marched us to the Parker Hotel to get on the bus to Cincinnati. After we arrived at Cincinnati we were taken directly across the river to Fort Thomas, KY. Fort Thomas was an old military establishment, had been used as early as the Civil war, the buildings were old and dilapidated. There we took the oath of office and were given a physical and our clothes. We filled out papers about our background and our education and took two tests, an aptitude test and a mechanical test and some one evaluated those and decided what type for service we were best suited for. Darned if I didn't do well. It haunted me the rest of my life! Then we were ready to be transferred out all over the country for whatever type of training they were going to give us.

It was real cold that winter and it was quite something new for me to leave home and be sent into the Army- start operating under Army rules, the different food, eating in the mess hall, reacting to orders, beginning to understand what discipline was. When I entered the Army, my pay was $21 a month. Ten dollars went for insurance, and we had to pay fifty cents a month to support the old soldiers home. Laundry was 75 cents, beer was a nickel and cigarettes were a nickel a package.

After two days, I was sent out to Fort Knox, Ky. At the time, it was the center of the armored branch of the service. We were sent out to the training areas then placed in barracks in groups of 210, what they called a company at that time. A day or two later, we began our training in armor. Our company was to be trained in the use of half-tracks and tanks. Our equipment was certainly rather antique compared to what are you're used to seeing today. The tanks and half-tracks burned what you'd called diesel today, but in those days it was not much better than coal oil. Every morning, especially with the tanks, before we'd start out we'd have to build fires under them and warm up the fuel tanks underneath to get the motor started. Many times we'd have to push them to start before we could begin the day's training.

We spent ten weeks there training basically in maintenance, use of the tank, military planning. We learned the basics of small arms, rifles and pistols, along with the physical training every morning which is still pretty much the same today as it was then. Near the close of the training, ten of us were called in as possible candidates for officers school. Six were picked; I was not one of them!

At that time, instead, I was contacted by Bill Lukens, who was the camp veterinarian at Ft. Knox. He was taking care of game warden duties at the preserve. He asked if I wanted to join that group and work at that, so I transferred to headquarters company at the administrative end of it and attached as a member of the veterinary corp. For a while I worked and lived out in the country with another fellow in a house, acting as game wardens, protecting wildlife. That seemed kind of boring, and before long I decided I wanted to do something different for the war than be a game warden. So I asked headquarters if they had some other kind of job for me. One day they asked if anybody in the outfit could type. I told them I could, though I didn't tell them I was really slow at it. So they brought me back into headquarters. There I went into the administrative section as a morning reports sergeant, making out the daily reports with all changes of status of every individual in the camp.

It was the first lucky move I made during the war. Like everyone, in addition to my daily duties, I was required to stand guard one or two nights a week. On Easter morning, 1942, when the 13th armored regiment moved out of camp Knox for overseas, I was standing guard. A lot of the men I'd trained with were in that group, moving out to the east coast to be put on boats and sent over to Africa. A few days after reaching North Africa, they were sent in to the line at Bayou Pass, at night under cover of darkness. When they woke up, there were batteries of German 88's pointing down their throats. The troops were all taken prisoner and spent the entire duration of the war as prisoners of war. If I'd gone with them, that's where I'd have spent the war, too. That was my first lucky break.

I stayed at Ft Knox 'till about August of that year in the office as morning report sergeant, One morning I was called in and told they were building a cadre to go to Camp Breckenridge, Kentucky. The cadre was to be the first 50 enlisted men going into this new camp. I was picked to go operate within the S-3 section of the new camp, detailed under Major Leonard Marksbury, a former policeman from Dayton, OH. We began preparing ourselves to be transported down to Camp Breckenridge to start the new camp, Within six weeks were sent down, but when we arrived there was only one barracks that had been built so far. They were just beginning to build up this camp, although it was being built up rapidly. This was down around Morganfield, KY. My job was range sergeant, to prepare the rifle and artillery ranges for the incoming new trainees. It was going to be used as a camp to train infantrymen.

We lived in good conditions for about the first two months, until the first men began to come in. I was an enlisted man, but we'd go into Evansville, Indiana at night, we'd go into one of the better restaurants in town and all you had to do was sit down and some civilian would come around and pick up the check. At that time, there were so few soldiers in the area, everyone was respected and looked up to. After the influx of infantrymen were moved into the area, it soon got to the point where we weren't respected as much, and so were kind of on our own after that. I stayed there for several months as range sergeant or S-3 sergeant, but I decided I didn't care for that as much as I thought I would. When I made Staff Sergeant, I was making $75 a month.

While I was down there, I did become a mason. I'd started my mason work back at Lodge 919 at Fort Knox, at least partly because my commanding officer was a mason. After I gained my first degree, I was transferred to Morganfield, and got my third degree there. I paid my dues every year after that but never went to another meeting after leaving Kentucky.

One day in the mail at HQ, I noticed an announcement for an opening for one person in the 5th Corps area in the horse cavalry at Fort Riley KS. The 5th corps covered about five or six states, but I made the application any way, and couldn't believe I was chosen. There was only one opening and I got it! It meant I was also accepted as a candidate to the cavalry's officer school at Fort Riley, KS. Fort Riley was the center of the US cavalry. I didn't know what I was getting into.

February 22, 1943 exactly one year to the day from the time I was mustered into the Army, I began Officers school at Fort Riley, KS. I'd never ridden a horse too much, except the old plug horses we had around the farm, so I had to learn all the ways of horsemanship. In my class, there were a lot of sports figures and celebrities and and most of the men came from very wealthy families. They had all been horsemen in their own right. Some of them were so wealthy they'd even brought a string of their own polo ponies with them to use at Fort Riley.

One was Pat DiCicco who was an agent and movie producer as well as an alleged mobster working for Lucky Luciano. He was married to Gloria Vanderbilt. He'd been her agent before they married in 1941 but they divorced in 1945 I helped Pat with his lessons. There was Oleg Cassini, the couturier, or dress designer, from New York and Ed French, a polo player from Canada and a fellow named Burnsley, a polo man

13

from England. All of them had some connection to racing or polo or horse breeding. I roomed with Dan Dailey, the dancer and actor, for the first six weeks. Even though he was famous, he never bragged one time. After the war, he went back to making musicals in Hollywood and recording songs with the Andrews sisters.

On weekends Hollywood people would come down and visit their friends in the army. I remember one day Gene Tierney often came to lunch. One woman who visited wore diamond rings on her thumbs.

I was kind'a out in the cold as far as being a good horseman but I was able to hold my own, although it was difficult. I never had any trouble with the academics. We had study hall just like a school, and sat at a long table learning military strategies. My biggest trouble was with the horsemanship. But after ten weeks, we were graduated 2nd Lieutenants- I made it! And was immediately transferred to what we called the Republican Flats at Ft. Riley, the area where all the training took place. I was placed in the administrative school area, teaching administrative duties and all types of office work that pertained to the Army. I trained two groups and was starting on the third group when I was transferred.

While I was at Ft. Riley, Isabelle and I got married, in September of 1943. I couldn't take time off, so Isabelle had to do everything-get the license, find a place to live. She was used to managing things, though. She had graduated from Bliss Business College and she had a good job with Farm Services, a very responsible position out of Columbus. She was one of just four women in the state who had that job. They covered 88 counties and did a lot of good, helping tenant farmers buy small farms and a team or horse or cow or two. She drove all across the state by herself and made $1440 a year. The government paid for mileage but each of the ladies owned their own car. Over the years, we'd often meet people she had helped, people that were successful and had gotten started with Farm Services and her assistance.

When both of Isabelle's brothers went into the Army, her parents, who were just in their 50's, insisted that she come home and help them take care of the farm. I don't think there are very many women who would do that, quit a good job and go help their folks, but she did. That's how it was then. She was taking care of their farm when she joined me at Republican Flats.

Isabelle was a virgin when we got married. The morning after our wedding night she said, "Well, I don't know what the big deal was about that."

We thought we'd have at least six months before I was shipped out but we just had three weeks. I got orders and was transferred to Camp Lockett, California to join the 10th cavalry. There was quite a bit of history associated with the 10th. It's one of the oldest regiments in the Army, a segregated, black regiment formed in 1866, following the Civil War. The enlisted men were black and the officers were white, which was typical at the time. The army didn't integrate until 1948, under Truman. The 10th fought Cochise and Geronimo in the Indian Wars; they fought with Custer. I wasn't quite sure about my new situation; I'd never been around many black people.

We went by train from Kansas City to Camp Lockett, California. It was two and a half days, but we had to stand up all the way. Because of the war, old railroad cars used during the Civil War had been brought out of moth balls, they had gas lights and really hard riding. When we arrived in Los Angeles, we transferred to a little train that made it down to the border of Mexico. At Camp Lockett, I had a lot of duties, but I was a horse shoe inspector for the first month, in charge of making sure all the horses were shod. We had over 5000 horses at the camp. Then I was made assistant personnel officer. I had trained under the head of the personnel department at Fort Riley, so we had good rapport. I slept at the bachelors officers quarters and spent my time doing whatever they wanted me to do. I was just a fair horseman, not really good at all, so I was stuck mostly in administration. Part of the time, we'd ride the border; we'd send out patrols around platoon size, about 30 men and horses, and ride the border trying to keep Mexicans from crossing the border. But, most of my time, though was spent in personnel. I didn't get to be a line officer until I was six months overseas.

This was an old line outfit and the chances of promotion were hard to come by. However, we were only at this camp about 6 months, and in the early part of January 1944, we got orders to go overseas; the whole 2nd Cavalry Division was being sent to North Africa.

The horse division was dismounted, because horses weren't going to be used in the war. Before leaving, the unit held a retreat, the last one of an of an old line horse cavalry. It was a beautiful thing, We had a mile oval, like a race track. For their first pass around the track, the horses, all 5000 of them walked, four abreast. For the second pass, they cantered, eight abreast. For the third time around, we galloped around the track, sixteen abreast. You can imagine the grandeur of 5000 horses, perfectly groomed, perfectly calm, handled by men in military dress, in full gallop. It was a beautiful sight.

We left Camp Lockett in January and then began a long ride across the US in a troop train. It took us ten days to reach Patrick Henry on the coast of Virginia, our jumping off point for the trip across the Atlantic. Patrick Henry is built kind of on a swamp, it was cold and damp; water was everywhere. all the walkways and tents were built above the water. It was a cold, messy time. We were there several weeks, for physicals, shots and all the necessary paperwork before we were ready to be sent out.

CHAPTER 3

Building Bridges

We were transported to Africa on a brand new ship, the Billy Mitchell, a ship built especially for the war as a troop ship, but that would be converted later to a cruise ship. The Billy Mitchell was 623 feet long, 76 feet wide; and a cruising speed of 19 knots. There were 5000 men for that maiden voyage, if you can imagine that many people on one ship. We were packed in pretty thick. The men down in the hold, the enlisted men, slept 4-6 deep; they slept on top of each other. In the officers area, there were 20 of us in a cabin that was intended to hold two people in peacetime.

We were ten days crossing the ocean. I must admit I'm a poor sailor - I got seasick before we got outside the limits of the continental shelf. To make matters worse, I was made mess officer and had to spend most of my time, at least eight hours a day, down in the galley keeping order and making sure the men were fed. Anytime I could get off duty, I'd run up and get outside for a breath of fresh air. I was sick at my stomach from when we started until we landed at Casablanca. Still, I'll never forget what a beautiful sight it was as the ship moved into the harbor when we arrived off the coast of North Africa or the gold leaf roofs of the Sultan's buildings.

We marched about five miles from Casablanca to a camp maintained by the Moroccan government for the US called Don B Passage. On the way, we went right through the part of town where all the camel caravans came in. I suppose there were hundreds, thousands of camels there. The camel caravans came in from the desert with goods to be sold at the Casablanca bazaars. I was amazed at how beautiful the buildings were and how well they were built. They were all done in the old Moorish architecture. Even their apartment buildings were so much nicer than what you'd find here in the US, at least on the outside, and everything was white with red tile or gold leaf roofs. It was a very beautiful city.

However, down in the bazaar area, there were a lot of smells and odors from all the camels and all. It was the first time I'd ever seen Arabs. The Arab men were very swarthy, all wearing their turbans and long robes. Most of the men chewed betel or betel nut and the saliva from chewing the betel ran down the side of their mouths as red as blood. It was an unusual sight to see.

Camp Don B Passage, supposedly named after the first American Soldier killed in the African Invasion, was a combination Replacement and Staging Area, southeast of Casablanca, contained in barbed wire enclosure approximately one half mile square. It was tremendously hot there. The heat from the desert just settled in, but they were good accommodations. Outside the camp, and all around it, were were tents set up by the nomadic people who came to do business in Casablanca. The night we arrived, we received orders that no one was to leave the camp and told that the Arabs would kill us for our clothes or whatever we might have. The next morning we came up short 40 men and made a search of the camp area. We found them. They'd all had their throats slit and been thrown in a dry well with their clothes taken. It wasn't long after we got there that we realized just how many men had been lost or had sold their clothes, because almost every Arab had at least one piece of clothing that was US Army issue. They got hold of it by killing someone or bartering with a soldier.

After a week or so at Don B Passage, they loaded us on a train to Oran. It was the first and only time I had the privilege, if you could call it that, of riding on a 40 & 8 car. During WWI, the boxcars that transported Americans to the front could hold either forty men or eight horses, so the numbers 40/8 were stenciled on their sides. This uncomfortable mode of transportation was familiar to anyone who fought in the trenches and a common small misery among American soldiers. The only thing in the boxcar was a lister bag, a canvas water bag used especially for supplying military troops with chemically purified drinking water. If you hadn't been able to scrounge around or get issue, you were without food-and there were no restroom facilities. If we hadn't stolen a big can of Spam, we'd have starved! The train moved at the tremendous speed of 5 miles an hour. We went 1000 miles from Casablanca to Oran over the Atlas Mountains and it took five days and nights to make that trip. By the time we reached the half way point, up in the top of the Atlas mountains, we were beginning to get mighty hungry. Finally, they stopped and let us unload out of those cars and fed us creamed chicken and rice. I admit there were many feathers in the creamed chicken but it tasted mighty good because it was the first meal we'd had to eat in two and a half days.

It was interesting traveling through the country. The few people in that area lived in huts that looked like inverted cones on stilts, called, krales. People were very poor, the vegetation sparse because the rainfall was sparse, and the farming was elemental. There were groups of goats that they raised for meat and milk. There weren't too many people, but there were small villages every fifteen miles or so.

Oran is a big city, a seaport city. We were broken up into groups in Algeria. There we were placed in pools, an enlisted men's pool and an officer's pool, waiting to be reassigned. It was a place of extreme boredom. There was no place to go- you just ate and slept and waited to be assigned. At that time most of the frighting was going on up in Italy, especially in the Anzio area. The officers would go to the bulletin board every morning. They were sending about sixty 2nd Lieutenants in a plane to Italy each day to lead patrols at Anzio. It was clear they were being knocked off at that rate, about 60 a day, being killed or injured and had to be sent back. So those of us who were 2nd Lieutenants were really sweatin' it out. Every morning you'd rush out to the bulletin board to see whether or not your name was up and you were going to Anzio.

I got lucky again.

One day I was walking around the compound and ran into a fellow I knew as Taco. He'd been in charge of administration at Fort Riley, Kansas and I'd taught under him there at the clerks school. When he told me he was personnel officer there at the camp, I said, "Can't you find me a job?" He asked me what I could do and I said, "I can do anything- I don't want to go up to Anzio if I can help it!" He said, well, they were getting ready to form two new engineer battalions, two bridge battalions and asked, "Are you an engineer?" I didn't hesitate. I told him, "I'm the best engineer you ever saw!" Of course, I didn't know anything about engineering, and he KNEW I didn't now anything about engineering, but he said there was one opening in one of these battalions for an adjutant, the administrative man for the group. He said "I'll see what I can do. The next morning, he called me in and gave me my assignment as adjutant of the battalion. I suppose that was the second luckiest thing that happened to me in the war. If not for him, I'd have probably gone to Anzio and had a very short tenure as a soldier in the war.

A few days later, the new group was brought together and sent out about 20-30 miles west and south of Oran to the town of Mostaganem, Algeria, a town of about 10,000 people. We began drawing equipment and forming the new battalion, the 1553rd pontoon Battalion. We were to train on the Chelif River, a river that came out of the Atlas mountains and emptied into the Mediterranean Sea. It was an excellent spot to do our training. We spent about three months, learning a new business and establishing our schools to train the men in engineering, bridge construction and heavy equipment maintenance. We had a lot of heavy equipment. I remember each company had 62 semis and we had a total of 126 vehicles of all kinds. We had bulldozers and cranes - all types of heavy equipment to be used in bridge construction. All this had to be learned because none of the men -or the officers themselves- had been trained in that type of work. Our battalion had seventeen officers. The officers also had to learn the basics of engineering, so they could construct bridges under a variety of conditions. For months, we trained making floating bridges until we could build them in the dark.

It was a period of intense training but we had some other interesting experiences, too. One of our officers, a fella named Weeks, got acquainted with the Mostaganem Military Governor. One night I was invited with him to the governors home. The military governor, his name was Krusberg, was strong politically in that area. He was in his middle sixties, his wife was Spanish, they had a beautiful home with 6-7 Arab servants. I remember going into the drawing room and all along the walls he had animals, the trophy heads of animals he'd shot on Safari farther south in Africa. The night when we had dinner, it took three and a half hours to complete.   They'd bring one course at a time. They brought the first course, and I dug in, but the captain leaned over and whispered, "You don't want to do that. You won't be able to eat through the whole thing. You just want to eat a little bit of everything that comes along." We had started with aperitifs and we had all types of wine and ended with a digestive, a thick viscous wine they served in a goblet about the size of a thimble. That was the first time I'd ever eaten in an elegant setting, eating a whole dinner under those type of conditions, with the Arab women servants standing there waiting to replace the wine or anything else you might need. Never thought dinner could take more than three hours to finish. It was high class living! I visited him several times afterwards but that dinner was memorable.

After weeks of training, we got orders to ship to Italy. With all the equipment, it was a big problem, all the semis and vehicles and building materials. It was a mammoth job to move all that equipment. We had to send all our trucks and heavy equipment up to Bohn, about a thousand miles east of Oran, along the coast. We split into two groups, the one that was taking the equipment to Bohn loaded onto LST's and were taken across the Mediterranean to Italy. The rest of us were loaded onto a big English ship in Oran, several thousand of us. We arrived several days ahead the equipment.

While we were on that Limey ship, we had only two things to eat- boiled fish and kidney stew. The odor of kidney stew permeated the ship, that's all you could smell all the time, kidney stew a-cooking. We were 3-4 days crossing the Mediterranean but the water was perfectly calm; the water just looked like a glass mirror. Ten or twelve LST's were sent with us on the same convoy. They were carrying Arabs and Sikh fighters from India. The order was given that there would be no stopping for anyone who went overboard. I'll never forget when someone on the ship behind us was either thrown over or jumped or fell overboard; they never stopped for him. You could see him back in the distance as we moved on ahead, thrashing around in the water. Of course, we were out hundreds of miles in the sea so I know he never made it.

CHAPTER 4

Chateaus and Champagne

Eventually we landed at Naples, Italy and were unloaded. We had to walk through Naples about six or eight miles out to the suburb, Bagnoli. We were quartered in a potato patch, if you will, with olive trees scattered around in the potato patch. That's where we were to bed down with our pup tents and all. That evening, though, some of our black enlisted men went into town and they got into a fight with some of the white infantrymen, also our own Americans. They got into a fight, and back came the blacks, and at the same time, behind them came the white infantrymen who started shooting at us. We spent the whole night with our noses buried in the dirt with rifle shots going over the top of our heads. It wasn't until we could get help from headquarters that we could stop the infantrymen shooting at our blacks. I'll never forget my first night in Italy, with my nose buried in a potato patch where the potatoes had just been dug out a few days before.

In our unit, all the enlisted men and warrant officers were black. They were some of the nicest guys I ever met and some of the worst. There isn't much fraternization between officers and enlisted men, but I was often in the position of hearing about some of their experiences, which could be very different. One of the black sergeants got a letter from his wife about how she had been assaulted in her home by a local white man. He felt so bad that he couldn't do anything about it so far away, and that maybe he couldn't have done much if he'd been there. He explained it, "Your house is your house all the time, but mine isn't." That's a hard thing for a man to take. I didn't know what to say to him.

In a few days, the rest of our group came from Bohn in LST's with our equipment, and we moved to Caserta, on the Volturno River, 25 or 30 miles north of Naples. We stayed in that area training for several weeks. By that time, the heaviest fighting had ended at Anzio and Monte Cassino, so American troops began moving north toward Rome along the highway. Our job was to build bridges for them whenever they came to a place where they had to cross the river. We bridged up to the Volturno River at Rome then we were pulled back for regrouping -and some rest.

That's when I went to Rome for a weekend with Captain Andrews. We spent three days and got to see all the historic landmarks of the city, we stayed at Continental Hotel. It was a very exciting and interesting weekend, staying in a city the size of Rome, going around and seeing the Coliseum, and all the cathedrals, especially, the most important thing I got to see, St. Peter's Cathedral. It's a beautiful thing. They started building it in the 11th century. The fellow I was with was Catholic and he got us into places I wouldn't have known about. I got to see the Pope being carried on his sedan chair. We got into the Sistine Chapel to see all the beautiful paintings and works by Michaelangelo and statues by Bernini in the nave of the cathedral. Seeing St. Peter's Cathedral was an awesome, exciting experience.

After we came back from Rome, we remained at Caserta for a number of weeks, preparing for a landing in Southern France. In Caserta they showed us the place where the slave Demetrius stayed. Demetrius was the slave who supposedly got a'hold of the robe that Christ wore when he was taken down from the crucification. I couldn't tell if they really believed it or if it was just the story that went with the town.

On the 10th of December, 1944, we received orders to prepare for loading to go to southern France. After 2 days of loading onto LST's, we departed on the 13th under cover of darkness and proceeded up the coast the short distance, only a few hundred miles to St Tropez, France. St. Tropez is a beautiful beach located just beside Monaco, in the eastern part of France where it joins Italy. It took us two hours and forty five minutes to finish unloading. Those damn Navy boys were laughing because we wouldn't get our feet wet, so they dropped the lid in water up to our necks! There was no one there to greet us.

We proceeded to the command post, where we got all of our unit together ready for the movement north. On the morning of the 14th,

Colonel Shellenberger left with an advanced party en route to Dole, France to find a bivouac area. That morning we moved down the coast to Marseilles, a rather large city on the coast with a lot of movement of troops by the First French Army that had been down in Africa.

Along the way, we noticed some German railroad guns burning, so stopped to check them out. While we were looking, an automobile pulled up and a well-dressed man stepped out with a briefcase and asked if we would take him to General de Gaulle up at Valence, about 40 miles north of Marseilles. We were skeptical and actually had orders to not have anything to do with civilians because you never knew which side they were on, so we put him off and got back in our jeep. We stopped for something else and while we were standing there, the car came up again and this time the man got out of the car and said, "I don't imagine you know who I am, but I'm George Bidault, former Secretary of State for the French Government, returning from exile in Switzerland. I'm on my way to a meeting with General de Gaulle at Valence."

Naturally, we almost fell all over ourselves getting him into the jeep because he was an important personage! We started up the highway towards Valance, a real old city built by the Romans in the 11th or 12th century. On the way up, we came to a crossroads and our guest wanted us to turn right. He wanted to go to this little town called Tin. When we arrived at Tin, the local Maquis, the underground, were holding a celebration. The Maquis were rural guerrilla bands of French Resistance fighters. They had just taken that town a day or two before, so they were real happy to see Bidault and they put out the red carpet for him. They made a big fuss over him and had a parade. We led the parade in our jeep. After the celebration was over, he insisted we go to a certain café. So we drove down to this well-worn, old café, and the lady that ran it was all excited because Bidault was there. She gave us an excellent dinner and brought out a bottle of wine she said was over a hundred years old, in honor of Bidault being in her café.

We spent the whole of that night with the French Maquis in Tin. They carried on something awful. They were rather rough individuals;

they'd been fighting underground against the Germans for about two years. It was clear the Maquis didn't like us, so I told the colonel we should probably go. We were sitting at a long table with them drinkin' and a'carryin' on and I had a great idea. I'd taken French in high school, so I stood up and led the group in the French national anthem. I sang right along with them. We had quite an exciting evening but woke up the next morning sick as dogs. That's the only time I ever got drunk.

Before he left, Bidault gave us a letter of introduction, that we were to use if we were in areas where friends of his might live. We were glad of it later on when we were welcomed at a number of fancy chateaus while the other soldiers had to sleep outside. Many a night the colonel and I slept between sheets, when the other men were roughing it.

The next morning, we left early, going north and arrived at Dole. It's about halfway up in France, an older city with about 10,000 people. We selected a bivouac area in the woods. After getting it approved by headquarters and marked off, the colonel and I returned to meet the battalion that had already come north about as far as Lons-Le-Saunier. The next morning, on the 18th, we moved up into Dole, France, arrived at our bivouac area and set up our unit in the woods to stay awhile, awaiting orders to move forward as was needed in the operation.

On the 19th , it was discovered that the little town of Auxonne, near Dole, had a railroad siding with a German pontoon bridge on railroad cars that had been ready to move up to the front but had been captured. The general in charge of that area gave us orders to get that pontoon bridge off those cars and set it up so we could get some idea of how their bridges were in case we ever wanted to use them if we captured any later in the war. That day we spent unloading the five railroad cars , hauling it to our bivouac area. We set it up in an open field, because we didn't know how to put it together, and we wanted to use it for study. For the next two days, we tested the bridge set-up so the generals could do some evaluating.

We completed the salvage on the 22nd of September and on the 24th, we received orders to prepare a bridge and ferry school on the

Doubs River for other engineering units so they'd know how to build a bridge if was needed. The training took about four days, and on the 27th, company B constructed a pontoon bridge across the Mozelle River at Pouxeux, France, and supported the 36th Armored Division. This was a very effective bridge and we were able to move the division over and aid in the movement of the front. In the operation, we were called upon, first of all, to move a battalion of infantry across the river to set up a bridgehead to protect us while we built the bridge. We did this each time. One of our companies carried a "storm boat" section which consisted of 16 storm boats each with 55- horsepower outboard motors that carried ten soldiers plus the operator. The storm boats were 30'x8', four feet deep. We sent the infantry over first to cover us while we built the bridge. So we ferried across around 600 men before we even started the operation of building the bridge.

On the 5th of October, we moved to a garage in Dole. From the time we'd arrived in France it had been steadily raining. We were quartered out in the woods, but it got was almost impossible to exist out there in the dampness and men were getting sick. We found this big garage in Dole and moved the unit into it. Now, we were carrying around 600 men plus all the equipment so it took quite a large area for us to move into, with our kitchens and so forth.

October 6, I was busy with administrative duties, getting our rations set up and our communications with the different headquarters and the corp set up. On the 10th the ladder companies went to Valbonne for bridge training on the Rhone River, which was quite a large river.

In the meantime, on the 8th, thanks to our letter of introduction, we became acquainted with some wealthy people that lived in the Château de Verriere in Le Veille Loye, a little town outside of Dole. We went that evening and had dinner with them. The son in law was the secretary of agriculture for the French government before the war and had the exclusive rights for making all the champagne bottles in France. It seems that all the well-known families in France had exclusive of some kind, one family had the exclusive for making the paper for all the money in France. The government would give the families exclusive contracts.

At Christmas, 1944, we were at the château. I don't know what gave her the notion, but the grandmother, who was about 60, decided she wanted to go see her parents, who were in their 80's in Epinal, about 125 miles from where we were. Her family had the Champagne franchise; they were known as the Champagne Kings of France. They had champagne caves with thousands of bottles of champagne and every six months, they gave each bottle a quarter of a turn. It was Royet champagne. She talked us into taking her to see her parents and the colonel agreed to let me go. We took off at dark in the command car; she knew the roads. We traveled all night and even crossed into German lines to get there but we stayed three days, being wined and dined for our efforts. I had to bring her back at night too, but her folks loaded the car with 15 cases of champagne so it seemed worth the risk.

Hauling a civilian, outside my area, carrying champagne, breaking all kinds of rules. If anyone had ever caught me, I'd have never seen daylight again!

For about six months, we trained French troops in the use of 50 caliber machine guns, heavy machine guns used extensively as a vehicle weapon and for aircraft armament, and in 81 mm mortar, a medium-weight, muzzle-loading, high-angle-of-fire mortar used for long-range indirect fire support to light infantry and air assault units. We got to Paris twice. It had been declared a free city when the French government fell, and I saw as much as I could at the Louvre in a very short time. The bread in Paris was the greatest. Everybody carried around these long loaves of bread.

I was married so I didn't mess around like some of the others. Even though I was the second youngest in the outfit, and usually the youngest in the group, since I didn't need to go into town, I was officer of the day most of the time. I wasn't an angel-I drank hard liquor over there, mostly because they don't cool their beer! And, I liked their cognac. In Europe, those people drink all the time and never get drunk, but you can't have liquor around Americans. We went to the place where the monks made Frangelico, the hazelnut liqueur. They said we could get some but I'm sure they regretted it. Our bunch went overboard and had quite a bit more than just "some". After the war I'd drink a double bourbon when we'd go to dinner, but I haven't had a drink in 20 years.

CHAPTER 5

The Colmar Campaign

Then it was back to the fighting. On the 28th of October, we moved to Fort du Bambois, two miles south of Epinal. Fort du Bambois was an old fort from WWI. It was sunk into ground into the side of a large hill, totally protected from artillery but it was cold and damp. We had difficulty cleaning it up and setting it up as a headquarters or as a place for men to stay, but it was better than being out in the rain. They didn't want us to remain at the garage too long because we were kind of sitting ducks if there was an air raid. On the 6th of November, Brigadier General Garrison Davidson, our commanding officer in charge of engineering, made an inspection. He awarded the battalion the Soldier's Medal commendation for our state of discipline and training.

General Davidson had been chief engineer for the Seventh Army, serving under Patton in North Africa and Sicily. Patton used one of his own general stars for Davidson's battlefield promotion to brigadier general. "Gar" Davidson was commandant at West Point before the war started. After the war, he served as president of the first Nuremberg War Crimes Tribunal for military defendants.

November 7th through December 1st was devoted to general duties. The weather had been very disagreeable with snow all the time and quarters inadequate for comfort. The snow had been so heavy the front had become static and wasn't going anywhere. We were just waiting for orders.

It's hard to understand but war didn't happen all day, every day. But, the worst part of war wasn't the fighting; it was the weather. If you got wet, you couldn't get dry. If you got cold, you couldn't get warm. It hurts so bad when you get cold and wet and we never could get dry. It was stormy and freezing cold going over the mountains in the winter of 1944. Once, I was counting the men as they came over and saw a little building with smoke coming out of the roof. When that last vehicle came over, I ran to that building. There were fifty soldiers piled around the stove. I just dove on top top them, I didn't pay any attention to the other soldiers, I laid there till I warmed up.

On the 3rd of December, I assumed command of Company B; I had been the adjutant. After a few days of problems getting them organized again, I became the new company commander. On the 5th, we held bridge schools for all the new combat battalions that had arrived. It snowed and rained constantly. On the 15th, we began road maintenance. The roads were almost impassible and the front had stalled so we began the job of opening up 200 some miles of roads. With heavy snows 2-3 feet deep and all the ice, it was quite a task. We had to bring in big shovels-they weren't steam shovels, they were run by gasoline motors-and 185 dump trucks.

We found a spot where they'd been manufacturing roofing tile and they had a 3-4 acre field of cinders. We used the cinders to put on the roads. They were very effective-within a few days we had the roads perfectly cleared. We got a commendation for it. This was in the area of St. Die, Baccarat, Rambervillars, Badonville, Raon-l'Etape and Pexonne. We were charged with maintaining the roads in the middle of those mountains.

On the 18th of December, we began conducting schools in bridge construction and ferries. We did this till the 23rd of December for a week or ten days. It was very inclement weather. It was a difficult time to have schools and build bridges on these rivers with all the ice and cold. However, the rivers didn't freeze over because they move very swiftly in France. They have tremendous fall, so there's very little ice forming on the rivers because of the swiftness of the water.

On the 24th , I went back for the evening at the Château de Verriere for Christmas. On the 26th, we were still conducting schools. By then, we'd moved into a cement factory in Pouxeux, France. It was a rough place to be, as we found out shortly after they began stealing from us. They stole several hundred cans of gasoline and an outboard motor or two before we found out what was happening to them. We had quite a problem there. Then on the 1st of January, we moved to Avricourt to begin road maintenance. It was a ghost town. Formerly there had been about 2000 inhabitants, but there was no one there now. The Germans had totally destroyed the little town. Minefields were everywhere and what houses were standing were booby-trapped. Of course the weather was bad and we had trouble locating the materials we needed.

A man and his wife were the keepers of the factory. They had two little girls. They were poor, my god they were poor! I'd take sugar and things for them to eat. They'd play games and get the most fun out of each other. I liked to take care of folks like that when I could. Once while we were gathering equipment we saw a cabin with smoke coming out of the chimney. I went over to warm up. The woman there was scared and had a baby. When I tried to give her 20 francs, she must have thought I had something else in mind but I spoke to her in French and then she took the money and I warmed up by the stove.

At the time we were working out of Pexonne with our equipment. The interesting thing about this town of Pexonne - there weren't any men in the town. The Germans had taken all of 'em either for slave labor or killed them for reprisals. No one lived in the town except women.

On the 19th of January we had another school, 22 horsepower motor and rafting school near Dinoze. Even in combat, even though you're in an operation, you're constantly having schools. When you're not fighting, why, you're having schools. It's hard to realize, but that's what we were doing.

On the 26th of January, we finished experimenting with loading Bailey bridges on our flat tops. The Bailey bridge is a type of portable, prefabricated, truss bridge developed by the British. It had the advantages of requiring no special tools or heavy equipment to construct. The wood and steel bridge elements were small and light enough to be carried in trucks and lifted into place by hand, without requiring the use of a crane. The bridges were strong enough to carry tanks and could bridge up to 200 foot gaps. Someone decided that in addition to our floating bridges, we also would have to put up Bailey bridges, so we had to figure out ways to rebuild our semi-trucks with flat tops. We didn't need level tops to haul our other equipment. We had to construct flat floors on top of them and then decide how we could load them efficiently so we could transport the Bailey bridge where it was needed.

On the 28th, we were attached to the 21st Corps. We unloaded all of our trucks with the floating bridge and loaded them up with Bailey bridge. On the 29th, we started hauling Bailey bridge to the front; the front had began to move forward. We began to use Bailey bridges because they were good for short stretches and small streams. On the 30th we arrived at St. Marie aux Mines and reported to Colonel Arrowsmith. That was the night we worked all night getting our trucks over the mountain. It was in the middle of the Vosges mountains; I'll never forget that night. The mountain range was probably 5000 feet up. We had a difficult time, with the bad weather and all, moving those trucks. A lot of the trucks blew motors; we had to hook two or three trucks together to get them over. Of course, we had to do it under the cover of darkness, with no lights in freezing weather. There was a tremendous amount of snow and ice and it was 10 degrees below zero.

The next morning, on the 31st, we got all the trucks over the mountain and set up a bivouac area on the opposite side, where the war was beginning to accelerate quite a bit. On that day, we dispatched a bridge to support the 75th Division that was crossing at Olheim. We also sent one bridge up to Ribeauville, where the front was, to support a division up there. No one got any sleep. On the 2nd of February, we still hadn't had any sleep. We were still getting trucks over the mountains, moving bridges as fast as we could, we couldn't get 'em fast enough. We had to send part of our trucks back to Luneville to get more bridge. It was really a difficult time.

On the 4th of February, we moved from Liepvre, east of St. Marie, by way of Sélestat and arrived at Ribeauville to take charge of a Corps dump. At the same time we were putting up bridges at Kyserberg and Ingolsheim, trying to keep the battle going. This became the battle of Colmar. It was an unusual battle; it was the approach to the Rhine River. There were two towns, Colmar and Sélestat. There was ten miles between them and the highway between them was perfectly straight. It was a nice big, wide highway. When the operation began, they caught the 19th German army on that road. It was a horse-drawn outfit; all their equipment was drawn by horses. They cracked the bridges at Sélestat and the one at Colmar. Because the roads had all been mined on either side, the Germans had mined it themselves, they couldn't even get off the road. Our planes just flew back and forth over that ten-mile stretch and just decimated that whole 9th Army. With ammunition blowing up and everything burning, people and horses, it was really a mess.

After the first assault we were ordered to move farther up and we were crossing small streams but we got caught by the Germans and they strafed us that night. Luckily, with the exception of a couple of men, we didn't lose too much more.

On the 6th of February Lieutenant Lind and I were moved to Neiderhergheim and Oberhergheim to bridge the Ill River. It wasn't too large a river, probably 150 feet wide, and the infantry was with us with the artillery a mile in the rear. It rained all night but both bridges were finished by dawn.

This was the place I saw an entire company of our infantry annihilated.

That morning we had just finished the bridges and were setting there, before dawn, eating breakfast around the campfire. This infantry company was with us. We were jokin' and kidding as soldiers do. About daylight their orders came to move out. They started moving down the road and they traveled about a half a mile to a crossroads. When they hit that crossroads - they were walking of course; they were infantry- the Germans opened up with mortars and artillery fire and just decimated those men, men we'd just been talking to a few minutes before. The attack must have killed about two thirds of them, a hundred or a hundred and fifty of them, in a matter of seconds. It was a terrible thing.

Afterwards I wrote up all the citations for every man who was getting an award.

CHAPTER 6

Crossing the Rhine

We were still moving bridges to the lines on the 10th of February-fourteen of them on that day. On the 11th we built a bridge at Neuf-Brisach. That was towards the end of the Colmar campaign. We'd been working with the 1145th Engineer group. By the 12th, the campaign was finished except for mop-up. You have to remember from the 28th of January to the 12th, we'd had little or no sleep, we were really busy moving all this equipment and building bridges. We got another job after that, to clean up the road from Sélestat to Colmar. We used two or three big bulldozers to shove burned equipment and dead horses off the road. We never counted, but there were thousands of dead horses on that ten mile stretch. You can't imagine the burnt horse flesh and the dead human flesh – and the odor.

With the campaign over, on the 19th we departed Ribeauville for Pouxeux and returned all our Bailey bridge to the 7th Army dump and reloaded all of our own equipment, getting ready for the crossing of the Rhine.

On February 20th, we detached from the 3rd Army infantry division and became a separate unit again. The next day we loaded our pontoon bridge in preparation for another combat bridge attack. The equipment was in bad shape. While we'd been at the front, the French had used our pontoons for target practice. We had to fix all the holes in the big pontoon boats. They were large boats- 32 feet long, 4 feet deep and 8 feet wide. We worked on them and patched them from the 24th to the 27th.

On the 27th of February, we built a 165 foot pontoon bridge across the Saar River, near Saarguemines, and we entered Germany for the first time. Minefields and booby traps were everywhere, making it very dangerous.

Sometimes when we were building bridges at night, we'd cheat a little. They'd send up white phosphorus bombs to give us some light. They would light up the sky for five minutes or so. But things always happen to slow you up. Once that winter we had a big blizzard with 3-4 feet of snow. The war had to stop-you can't fight in snow that's waist deep. We kept the roads open that winter, about 200 miles of it.

While we traveled, we had men called sappers, combat engineers who performed a variety of military engineering duties like bridge-building but also laying or clearing minefields, demolitions, field defenses and general construction, as well as road and airfield construction and repair. The term "sapper" comes from the French "sap", to dig or to trench. We were going to build a bridge across the Saar River, just a couple hundred feet or so, when our sappers found a few Teller mines and were digging them out. The Teller mine was a German anti-tank device with explosives sealed inside a sheet-metal casing and fitted with a pressure-actuated fuse. Because of its rather high operating pressure, only a vehicle or heavy object passing over the Teller mine would set it off. We didn't have time to defuse them and they had a built-in carrying handle on the side so I told the sergeant to stack them next to a nearby house. He didn't get it done. While our trucks were unloading the boats, they backed into the mines and exploded. The sergeant got blown up himself, as well as several other men and our crane. We had to unload the boats by hand and it took about forty men to handle each boat.

On the 3rd of March, we began hauling Bailey again for the front, 'cause things were moving fast. Of course, all this time, plans were being laid for the big crossing of the Rhine. On the 4th of March we moved from Neuvemaisons, ten miles south of Nancy, France, to hold another training school. Hard to think, but when we weren't fighting, we were constantly holding schools. At the same time we were doing a lot of experimentation in cable crossings and rafts. We were on the Mozelle River, living in French barracks with tile floors and all the comforts of garrison. On March 5th, we set up another training school on the Muerthe River south of Luneville, to train tank drivers in loading tanks on rafts and ferrying across streams. On the 12th, we were attached to the 40th Engineer group, in preparation of the assault on the Rhine River.

I was promoted to Captain March 16th. By this time, my pay was over $400 a month but I got so I'd only keep out 75 cents to spend and send the rest home. The other guys ragged me about it. They said, "Your wife will probably marry someone else when you get killed!" But, I saved my money anyway. Isabelle and I wrote to each other regularly, though not every day. Mail had to compete with food, fuel, ammunition and supplies for cargo space so when soldiers wrote home from the front, their letters were written on a special form. Each form was cleared by the censors for sensitive information and then photographed using 16-mm black and white camera film. The film reels with hundreds of letters were flown to processing centers in the addressee's general location. A copy of the letter would be printed and then mailed locally. During the war over 1.5 billion letters were processed like that.

The week of my promotion, we moved from Neuvemaisons back to Morhange. On the 18th we got five pontoon rafts ready for the big job, and got the bridge equipment ready for the Rhine crossing as well. On the 21st we moved to Oermingen.

That evening we were in Germany having to move at night under blackout to escape detection from German planes. We were bivouacked in the forest that night. On the 23rd, two days later, we departed for the Rhine, a 200 mile trip, under blackout. We passed through Kaiserlaughtern. Because there were so many convoys, the outfit was scattered all over the country. We arrived at Langmeil at dawn, ten miles from our bivouac area. To avoid detection, we were forced to hide our vehicles among houses and in buildings, all the time in danger of sabotage from the German civilians who were most hostile. At dusk on the 24th, we left our final assembly area near Dannefelds and arrived at the bivouac area. At last we had all our equipment together in place!

Crossing the Rhine was a major concern throughout the war because Americans knew the Germans would blow all the bridges. At every meeting, people would talk about how we were going to cross the Rhine.

On March 25th, we finally went on detailed reconnaissance of the river. Remember, we had been building up for the Rhine crossing, and training for it, during the entire past six months. We had 62 semi trucks carrying all of our material. You couldn't just run down to the lumber store to get supplies. After the reconnaissance, we watched from a command post, in a house just behind the levee of a bank, standing on the second floor we could look out over the river. We stood on one bank and Germans were on the other. While we were standing there in the house, trying to figure out the most effective place to build our bridge, our units were putting mortar fire across the river into the Germans.

The next day was the big day, the jump-off for the Rhine crossing. We brought in everyone.

On the 26th of March, at 2:30 in the morning, our storm boats carried the infantry across under heavy fire from flak wagons and small arms. After the first company of infantry went over, the Germans were throwing everything they could at us. I was bridge commander, which is like being a boss in a factory. Two in our group were seriously hurt in the first wave. One fellow had lost his arm and didn't know it until some asked him, "What happened to your arm?" Then he fainted.

The initial crossing was a success: the far bank was secured in about two hours. We began moving up to build the bridge, and commenced construction. We had to get a one inch cable across the river that was the same width as the Ohio River. It was a tremendous challenge. The Rhine is as wide as the Ohio River. We lashed the boats together and float them out to the cable. By 11:30, we had five rafts on the other side. We were short on construction personnel and everything went wrong but we still kept our schedule.

I was hit by cable about 4 o'clock that afternoon and didn't regain consciousness until midnight.

At 1 AM on the 27th, the bridge was finished, a thousand-foot bridge. We built the longest floating bridge on the Rhine River, 1062 feet. Only two outfits were doing this. The West Point group did the administrative bridges, but when they needed a combat bridge, they called us! We built a hundred feet an hour.

The armor began moving immediately. Sporadic gunfire from the German artillery kept us wondering, but no casualties resulted. Over 4500 vehicles, including 350 tanks, crossed our bridge that day. We honored General Gar Davidson by naming it the General Davidson Bridge. While the bridge was there, our maintenance personnel maintained it. We moved our company, B company, into a building at Rheindurkheim. We were about three miles north of Worms, Germany. Worms had quite a bit of history regarding the Protestant Reformation in the early sixteenth century. It was where Martin Luther made his protestant declarations against the Catholic church.

Bridge maintenance on the General Davidson continued through April but we went back and loaded up another bridge in preparation for another operation.

Long before the war, back at the farm, I used to have a recurring dream about being on a road and getting strafed. It wasn't anything I thought too much about, until one night not long after the Rhine crossing, we were moving trying to cross a bridge at night, pulling equipment with a bulldozer. About dusk, we heard a plane and he opened up on the road where the convoy was. I jumped in the creek and played out exactly what had always happened in that dream. The plane made three passes. I knew just what to do from that dream. It was like a drill performed over and over. I knew what was going to be said and what would be done. I don't have an explanation; when I talked about it later, people thought I was crazy.

On the 2nd of April, we moved to Heidelberg to take over the bridge across the Neckar River. Heidelberg was a beautiful town, a university town. It had escaped bombing during the war but when the Wehrmacht left the city, they destroyed three arches of the old bridge as well as the more modern bridge downstream. When the U.S. Army (3rd Infantry, 7th Army) entered Heidelberg on March 30, 1945, the civilian population surrendered without resistance. There's a huge park in the center of town and that's where we built a 250 ft. bridge to cross the Neckar and keep transportation moving until the engineers could come up and rebuild the old bridge or build a permanent one there.

The civilians in Heidelberg were very cooperative. I was made military governor for about a week there and we had put out orders that all civilian guns had to be turned in. I had a regular arsenal in my trailer with all the firearms turned in from civilians there.

On the 9th of April we left Heidelberg and returned to Rheindurkheim. On the 10th, we began dismantling the big bridge we'd built across the Rhine and hauled it and all the equipment, down to Worms, about three miles, and in the center of town in a big park there, made it a depot for all this equipment. We finished the next day and started moving across the Rhine to Darmstadt, Germany to an airport. This is where I saw I saw my first jet airplane. It was German, tiny- didn't have a wingspread of over 30 feet- just a small plane, but it was my first look at a jet plane.

On the 18th we left Darmstadt and arrived at Neustadt. On the 23rd we left Neustadt and arrived at Onolzheim. I was again made military governor of the city, since I was the ranking officer. That day I gave permission for five funerals to be held. On the 24th we were on the way to Wasseralfingen. At about 2 AM, we were caught by the Germans and they strafed us. Luckily it was dark enough they missed the main convoy, just strafed alongside it. I lost my first sergeant; he wasn't killed but both of his legs were blown off. My dozer operator was also hit, but not too bad.

We arrived at our new bivouac at 5 AM. On the 25th of April, we left Niederstotzingen for the Danube crossing. We had to go over some of the worst roads of the war, difficult terrain with a lot of swamps and places that were very difficult to get over. A lot of trucks upset and we had to work all night. We finally arrived at the bridge site at 8 AM on the 26th. We immediately constructed a 257- foot bridge across the Danube at Gunszberg in a 12 mile per hour current. Building time was three and a half hours. We had to build our bridge against another bridge that had been blown up by the Germans. The bridge had dropped into the river and partially dammed it, which increased the force of the water. Building in a 12-mile current was extremely difficult. Our utility boats were useless. We had 32-foot utility boats, with inboard continental motors, twin screws and they couldn't even push against the current so we had to do it all by hand. It was very difficult to get that bridge built by hand, but we did it, 257 feet in three and a half hours.

From the 27th of April through May 3rd, we were again hauling Bailey bridge wherever it was needed and also moved them from their last location up to the railroad station in Niederstotzingen. We were still maintaining the bridge on the Danube.

On the 4th, we left for Bad Tolz, Bavaria. Then I got as far as Landsberg, and of all places, we were billeted in a former concentration camp. The stench from the crematories was terrific but it was better than sleeping out in the sleet and rainstorm that had been going on for two days. This was our first look at a horror camp. It was like Auschwitz and Belsen. There were still a few Jews there, wearing the striped coats they'd been forced to wear by the Nazi's.

The next day, May 5, we left Landsberg and arrived at Bad Tolz. Vehicles and equipment were scattered all the way back to the Danube. We had bridged almost every river in France and southern Germany. The front was moving so rapidly, it was difficult to keep control of all the units and what they were doing. On the 7th we left for Rosenheim by way of Munich on the Autobahn. On the 8th, we were still hauling Bailey; we were quartered in an old schoolhouse but I was almost crazy with equipment all over and the difficulty of keeping track of it. You can see, everything was moving very, very rapidly

On the 9th of May, the war was over.

Everybody was happy.

CHAPTER 7

La Guerre Est Fini!

After the war ended, we were sent up to Belgium to gather the heavy equipment, cranes and earth movers that had been left all over Europe. On the 12th of May, we moved to the airport at Augsberg to begin getting all our personnel and vehicles all together.

The 13th was a very unlucky 13th. I don't remember if it was a Friday, but we lost a bridge. They sent us in to put in a bridge, not a big bridge, 200-300 feet. I got orders to go to Bavaria to build another bridge so I had a second in command take care of the Danube project. A commander in a tank, hauling another tank, dead head, pulled on to the Danube bridge. The bridge couldn't hold that kind of load. It broke loose and floated downstream about five miles to another blowed out bridge. I was called into headquarters and told I was about to be court-martialed because I'd lost a bridge. I was about 150 miles south of the bridge when it went out, but I was responsible for it; not just responsible, financially responsible. I thought I was going to spend the rest of my life paying for that bridge.

Nothing brings out the worst of bureaucracy like the chance to pass on blame to somebody else. With a lot of politickin' and the fact that the war was over, I eventually got off the hook but it took several weeks of sleepless nights and a steady stream of paperwork before that was accomplished.

I carried a weapon, a .45, during the whole war, but I never fired it. I couldn't have hit anything if I had fired it; I couldn't hit the side of a barn with that thing. I always figured if things got tight, maybe I could throw it at someone! In the horse cavalry, we'd carried short rifles, carbines.

On May 14, we moved to Gundelfingen and quartered in a machine shop.

Finally, May 31st, we moved into an area at Ulm, Germany to begin the salvage of that bridge that had floated downstream, turning in the equipment to a depot in Ulm. I tried to say no; I knew I would lose men. It was a place with a very fast current and a bad place in the river. I lost two men, drowned, in that salvage operation. I was quite disappointed in that because the war was over and to have men lose their lives after the war was over didn't seem right.

Ironically, on May 31st, I received a bronze star for my work at the battle of Colmar.

On the 1st of June we left for Reims, France, moving out of Germany. That night we bivouacked at Kaiserlautern. On June 2nd we arrived at Metz and we arrived at Reims the next day. On the 5th, we took equipment to Toul, France for turn in. On the 27th, for a period of time, we constructed flat beds for trailers and hauling equipment for the redeployment camps from Belgium to Holland. We gathered stuff from all over Europe, like cranes and earth movers. We were alerted for transfer to the Pacific and returned to Toul to draw all new equipment. We then went to Marseilles and made all equipment ready for Pacific shipment. On June 28th , we got orders to move to Camp Baltimore, there to prepare for deployment to the Pacific.

About a month later, after we'd spent all this time at Camp Baltimore getting ready for shipment, we were taken off the "ship" list and on the 29th of July, ordered to Chievres, Belgium to take over the equipment dump of the 181st Engineers and they took our place to go to the Pacific. On the 30th of July, we arrived at Chievres and quartered at the Château du Val, the most beautiful place we had ever been. We stayed several weeks, until September, when we were given the responsibility of building Camp Herbert Tareyton.

Like all the redeployment camps around Le Havre, Camp Tareyton was named after a cigarette brand. There was a Camp Lucky Strike, Camp Camel, all the popular brands. It had barracks and canteens so people could be quartered. It was a year bringing people back - no one was in a hurry after the war was over. They all had to come back by ship. Instead of being sent in units, we were being sent back as individuals according to the number of points. You got points from the number of days in combat, plus number of days overseas, plus number of awards, number of medals, number of battle stars - and how much room they had. Our unit had four battle stars; we got credit for four specific battles in the war in Europe.

In October, it was my time to be sent back to the states. We were along the English Channel and had loaded all the equipment on a ship similar to the one we came over on, the Billy Mitchell. It was too late to load the men, too dark, so they sent in truckloads of blankets, two blankets per man and we all went to bed. About 2 AM, the lights came on and everyone was cussing. The blankets hadn't been washed and they were infested with crab lice.

They brought in cans and cans of powder. We were not allowed on the boat until every man was treated. One of the officers was a minister who almost worried himself silly. He powdered himself about every hour.

They finally loaded us on the ship, about 5000 of us, and we headed back across the North Atlantic. This was a bad time of year, October-November, to be crossing the Atlantic! The ship was 35 feet high from bottom to deck and waves would regularly wash over the deck. One fellow got so seasick, for ten days the only thing he said was, "Oh, God, let me die!" I was sick on the way back, too. We landed at Camp Miles Standish in Boston. We stayed there one night and were sent to Indiantown Gap, Pennsylvania, where we were processed.

The war had ended in May and I got to come home in November of 1945. We bridged almost every river across France and Southern Germany, the Rhone, the Saar, the Rhine, the Danube in Austria, and dozens of rivers in between. From where I started, to where I ended up, I'd almost made a circle. Lots of people got killed during the war doing things and in places that had nothing to do with war, in houses or bars. I never felt like I had to tell the truth about that, though I have told some stories about them! I was lucky. We were in a lot of combat but I never got a scratch, except the time the cable hit me.

Isabelle picked me up in Columbus at the train station in the center of town. We went and had dinner. We acted like I'd just been gone a day or two and didn't think a thing about it. I started milking cows that night and got up the next morning at six in the morning to milk again. It was like I'd never been gone.

Still, it took a good while before I got the war out of my system. I'd go to sleep and have nightmares. It gave Isabelle fits. But, every body had them, the night mares. Everybody talked about it.

CHAPTER 8

Back to the Farm

All the time I was gone, Isabelle had saved all her money, too, so by the end of the war in 1945, we had $10,000 in the bank. We moved in with my parents and we all lived together until they died.

We produced just about everything we ate and had all we could do. We had a pretty good sized dairy; we bought milking machines pretty early on. I've heard people say, "Once you get in the dairy business, you don't live, you just dairy," and that's not far from the truth.

We also raised chickens, and turkeys, 400-500 turkeys each year for Thanksgiving. One year we cleared a dollar a head; we thought we were rich!

We didn't have children for seven or eight years - I was 30 when Jim was born. Both of our boys were born at the hospital- Jim cost $125 in 1950 and John was $150 in 1953. I knew from the records my father kept what the doctor's bill was when I was born - $15.

My mother had quit high school to marry Dad, but she was a great seamstress and was known as a good cook. Isabelle was also a good seamstress and a good cook so with both of them cooking and sewing, the house was like a little factory. No one came to the house to visit without leaving with something, a rug or a pie, something. Between the two of them, they dressed our children and grandchildren 'til the kids got big enough to insist on store-bought clothes, usually when they got to be 12-13. They kept a loom set up, too, and they made hook rugs and did cross-stitch. They sold some but they gave many of them away. Isabelle had a big vegetable garden beside the house and we ran a little truck patch. She planted flowers all around the house, too, especially hybrid tea rose bushes.

One day a week, Mom and Isabelle would do the washing, one day they did the ironing. Once a week, they'd make bread.

In the fall, they spent days and days canning and then butchering chickens and turkeys. We had caged layers, about 1200 of them, and

Isabelle would hang forty chickens on the clothesline, feet first, then cut their head off. After they'd bled out, the women would scald the birds in big pots of boiling water then pull the feathers off. It was a hard, messy business. The turkeys were worse 'cause they were bigger.

When we ran out of lye soap, they'd make some more 'cause we didn't want to buy soap when we could make our own. I blame Lifebuoy soap for making all that work for them. Nobody stank until Lifebuoy came along; everybody smelled the same, nobody knew they stank and it was okay.

We were always 'tight', careful with our money. We did everything ourselves, we didn't want to be paying someone else to do something we could do. There might have been easier ways to do things, and maybe we did things the hard way but that was our way. Most every day, I'd lift as many fifty pound pails of milk as came from the 40-50 cows that were fresh and dump them into the collection bin. I guess we could'a used a conveyor of some kind but we didn't have labor saving devices because they cost money.

I don't think there's any doubt we passed that sense of thrift on to the boys. We taught them to be careful about money.

My brother and his wife lived with our grandmother, Lewis's wife, Anna. Isabelle's parents lived on a farm about four miles away. It was about 105 acres. Isabelle took care of the old folks, her parents and mine, in addition to all the other things she did. Mom and Dad slept in the back bedroom, and we slept downstairs behind the kitchen. When the boys got too big to sleep in our room, we added a dormer and put in a room for them.

Everything on the farm was "joint" with Cedric and me. We each had 50% of everything, including each other's houses. We each kept records of what we spent and what we made and once a month, we'd get our wives and get out our spiral notebooks with all the disbursements and cash income and settle up. We'd hash out everything in the notebooks until it came out even. Sometimes he'd get a check, sometimes I'd get a check. We both kept laying chickens, Cedric and his wife also had 1200, and we both drew grain from the farm to feed the chickens, but the income from eggs and turkeys was separate. We had an arrangement with the Rainbow Bread man. He'd come and pick up several crates of eggs, 30 dozen to a crate every week. Isabelle had a weigher and she graded the eggs herself.

We managed two separate farms and we rented another. We raised feed - hay, grain, oats and spelt - plus seeds to use for future planting, like clover and timothy. I was always interested in trying new things. We were the first in the area to plant no-till corn. We even planted canola. We innovated but it seems like we always came back to the basics.

Some tasks changed with the seasons, but the work never ended.

We did the milking every morning from 5:30 to 7:30 AM. After breakfast, I'd lay out what was going to be done that day and how long each job would take. I'd be cussing and hollering when things didn't turn out just like I planned. Ced and I milked again at five in the evening. Our bulk tank handled 2500-3000 pounds per day. The milk truck would come from town every day to pick up the previous day's milk.

Like most farms, we always had cats around. They liked the milk, and we liked them around because they kept the rodent population down. There was one cat named Old Strainer Dish. We used a paper strainer, a six inch disc, to filter milk as it entered the bulk tank. We'd discard 'em when they got full. That cat would eat the whole piece of saturated paper, like a snake would swallow a mouse. But, what goes in has to come out, and that cat had figured out what to do. When the time came, she'd drag her butt on the ground to create traction to pull out that paper. She was really good at it!

My father used to catch black snakes and throw them into the barn. He said, "It serves two purposes. It keeps the rats out of the barn and it keeps the boys out of the barn". One of his favorite sayings was, "one boy is a boy; two boys is half a boy and three boys is no boy at all". There were five boys around the farm with Cedric's three sons and my brother and me. We got a lot of work done anyway.

'Course, when you have a farm, there's always plenty of work to be done. We raised Ayrshire cattle, Duroc hogs, chickens, turkeys and, in the late 1980's, Angora goats. Twice a week we cleared manure and then forked it into the manure spreader and spread it on the farm. We seldom needed any store-bought fertilizers! We also raised tobacco and broomcorn. Broomcorn is a coarse grass, grows 6-12 feet tall, that is dried and used to make brooms. It was a moneymaking project for the boys. They'd get it ready and we'd take it over to a blind man in Seaman who would make the brush into brooms. Normal broomcorn yields enough to make 150-350 brooms an acre.

We had only about a half acre in tobacco, but it was an important crop that took up a lot of time and effort. We'd put tobacco in around Memorial Day and harvest on Labor Day. Everybody helped with tobacco. The adults did the planting. Isabelle rode on the setter, transplanting the tobacco, along with someone else to help. I never rode the setter; I didn't have the patience. Every week or so, since we didn't use herbicides, the field had to be hoed. Once the tobacco got head high, it would shade the weeds but then the tobacco worms would get on it. The worms had to be removed by hand, by the men and boys. We'd use a tomahawk to cut the stalks, then impale them on a tobacco stick, a stake with a spear on top that was stuck into the ground. There were five stalks on each stick. It was hard work, and easy to get hurt doing it. The finished sticks weighed 30 pounds or so. We'd put them on a wagon and take them to the barn where they were spread out to hang on poles so they could dry. To help with drying, tobacco barns always had big doors for air flow and were painted black to keep in heat.

Around November, we'd take the tobacco to the stripping building, an old shed, really, where we had a disassembly line. It took four people. The first person cut off the first set of leaves, the second person took off the next layer, another person cut the third set and then someone cut the bottom. The boys did the tops and bottoms, the adults did the middle, the part that needed skill. The leaves were gathered and tied with an intact leaf into a "hand" and stacked on the tobacco stick, eight high.

You had to keep the leaves intact and make sure they didn't crumble. Then we put the sticks in our press, a handmade contraption made of plywood, for about half an hour. When it was ready, we stacked it up and Ced and I took it to Ripley, Ohio. Back then, all tobacco was sold at Ripley. The sellers would put it out in big baskets for the buyers to see. We never took the boys to the sale - there were too many bars and fancy women there. A lot of men got their tobacco money and then spent it all before they ever got out of town.

Ced and I both chewed tobacco so I made my own chewing tobacco from our crop. Store-bought tobacco hurt my teeth and it was always too sweet.

The boys started driving tractors when they were nine or ten. Besides school and chores, they had their own projects for making money. In the fall, they'd get home from school and head out to pick up walnuts. They had an old corn sheller to take the hulls off and they saved old pieces of roofing to spread the nuts out to dry. They'd bag them up in ragged old feed sacks, because we kept the good feed sacks to store feed. They'd take the walnuts to Peebles and sell them. The boys had school jeans and work jeans, the difference being school jeans weren't patched yet. Isabelle kept all the clothes going - she patched everything - and work jeans could always be mended.

I was always surprised that the boys didn't know how to do some of the things that needed to be done on the farm. I guess I figured they'd be born knowing how. Seems like I always knew what to do and they should, too. I must not have been very good at showing them but I didn't see how they could be so damn smart in some ways and so damn dumb in others. I wasn't very patient with them. I hollered at them just like I hollered at the men when we built bridges.

There were 40-60 cows to be milked twice a day, manure to be spread, eggs gathered, tobacco stacked, hay baled, vegetables to plant, grain to harvest, repairs made. We took care of pigs twice a day, fifty sows, from farrow to finish. We'd have 3-400 babies out in the woods. We made boxes for them to stay in and we'd take bags of feed and put in a feeder for them. After we bought the Donohoo farm, in 1968, we put in boxes for the pregnant mothers to have their babies and put in a finishing floor.

I always believed in punctuality, never saw any reason to keep anyone waiting or waste my time waiting for someone else. And, I also believed you shouldn't leave a job till it's done. The only exception to that was lunch and dinner. No matter what the job was, when it was time for dinner, we quit. The women were going to have food on the table that they had worked hard to prepare and we were going to be there when they served it. We had good food - pork chops, baked steak, fried chicken, stewed tomatoes, mashed potatoes and gravy, hickory nut pies, all kinds of pies, cakes and pudding. I usually had fried eggs, bacon and toast for breakfast with 2-3 glasses of milk. The family drank three gallons of milk a day.

Every morning before breakfast, I'd take an empty bucket over to the barn and bring back a full one from that morning's milking, carrying it across the 600-700 feet that separated the barn from the house. That's about the length of two football fields but I always walked it, never drove.

Our first truck was a 1949 one-ton Ford with a flat head V-8 engine. It was a good truck; we ran it every day. All the boys drove it, too. We kept it until 1972; you could see through the floorboards by then. The truck had Broadview Ayr Farms, M.R. and C.L. Surber & Sons painted on both doors. Ced did the driving but he and I went everywhere in that truck, spittin' and cussin'. We always opened the doors to spit tobacco. Ced chewed more than I did but we both chewed for close to eighty years. My dad chewed, too. He'd spit in the slop jar at the back door but I never did spit in the house. When I couldn't go outside anymore, I learned to just swallow. Didn't seem to do me any harm.

Of course, I smoked cigarettes during the war and for years after the war. Everybody smoked during the war. And, there was a time, when the boys were still small, I enjoyed King Edward cigars and went through a box a week. One day they just didn't taste good anymore and I gave 'em up. But I still chew.

Our family went to church Sunday morning, Sunday evening and Wednesday evening, except for my Dad. I usually led the singing. Except during the war, I bet I didn't miss ten Sundays at church in my life. I was a church elder for fifty years and taught Sunday school that whole time. I even had a radio program that was broadcast on Sundays for folks who couldn't get to church. A lot of people listened; there were sixteen Church of Christ churches in Highland County back then. Sometime before Jim was born, I accepted the job of putting flags on the grave sites of veterans buried at Union Cemetery. We'd put the flags out on the Thursday or Friday before Memorial Day. It became a family affair; Isabelle would read the names and the boys would help. I did it until I just wasn't physically able anymore.

I was president of the school board for a while but I was a teacher and a choirmaster at Union Church of Christ for years and a lay preacher when the preacher couldn't make it. I had a big voice, everybody wanted me to sing at their funeral! Isabelle played the piano at church and funerals, too.

During all the years we farmed together, Cedric usually drove the tractor and ran the baler, the combine and the corn planter; I did the stacking up in the barn in the mow. Ced would drive the tractor and I'd walk behind the thrashing machine raking up the corn till it was in a neat, knitted pile, ready for the cows to eat all winter. The dust would get so bad it would block out all the light.

We were only in our 40's the day I thought Cedric was dead. He was driving the tractor. We'd gone to the neighbor's on the tractor to borrow a post hole digger. Better to borrow one than buy one! There were four of us on that tractor, Cedric driving, me on one side of the tractor, two of Ced's sons hanging off the other side. It was actually a small tractor. Somehow, the post hole digger got caught in the road and bounced up and hit Cedric in the back of the head. The force of the blow knocking him forward bent the steering wheel in half. I was thrown off the tractor, which just kept going and ran over my legs. I chased the tractor till it went into the ditch. Cedric's eyes were open but glassy and he didn't speak. I was sure he was dead. I was glad to be wrong. Isabelle took him to the hospital to get stitched up but I didn't go to the doctor.

In the summer of 1970, I was around 50, and for reasons I can't remember, I took the combine out myself. Something didn't seem right and I jumped off to take a look at it. That old combine had steel bars that spun around and I must have been thinking about the cost of the repairs when I stuck my head under those flails and got a big gash in the head. I went back the house and sat down at the kitchen table. Isabelle put a towel around my neck and poured a bottle of iodine over my head. That hurt pretty good. Still, I got off lucky. About half the men in the community only had one arm because they'd lost the other one in a thrasher.

Around 1965, one of our show bulls, he was a national champion, broke through his paddock and got to me. He pushed right through those metal pipes like they were plastic. I broke 7 or 8 ribs and was purple from the waist up. After a few days of sittin' in the chair I decided I could get back to it. Didn't waste any money on a doctor then, either.

Cedric and I supported plans for the Highland County Fair grounds by becoming a founding member of the Fair Board. We helped clear the land for the fairgrounds and helped build the first livestock barn. Ced was active for 20 years or more. I just served 4-5 years - someone had to run the farm!

We showed our cattle all over the country. When the boys were old enough, they showed Ayrshires at the Highland County Fair, the Clinton County Fair and the Ohio State Fair in Columbus. Isabelle and I would go on the first day to help haul the animals and the gear, on the day they showed their animals and on the last day, to haul the gear and animals out. I guess we weren't exactly the hovering kind of parents.

Our oldest boy, Jim, was the first in our family to graduate from college, but we only went to see him three times while he was over there, to take him, to visit once when he was sick and the day he graduated. I know what I really needed to be doing on his graduation day was setting tobacco.

My son Jim and I argued the whole time he was in college, not about college but about Viet Nam. Every weekend he'd come home, we'd be into it; Isabelle and John finally got so they'd just leave the room when we started. We just couldn't see things the same way.

I think alcohol affected my Dad's interest in work, and he didn't spend much of his time doing it but the fall before he died in 1964, my father picked up a scythe and started cleaning fence rows. The neighbors were up in arms about, "Why are you making that old man work?!" We never knew what got into him, but he probably worked more in that six months than he had in the twenty years before.

My mother was diagnosed with cancer in 1950 and the doctor told her she would be lucky if she had a year or two to live. She died 26 years later, and although she didn't like to leave the house because of her colostomy and catheter, she was never one to just sit around. Mother read to my kids all the time. There wasn't that much to do for entertainment, but reading to them was the best thing she could do for them. After Jim got his driver's license, she did ask him to take her to the Colony Theater in Hillsboro to see "The Sound of Music" and she enjoyed that quite a lot.

CHAPTER 9

Day is Done

Cedric's boys left the farm when they got old enough. Both my sons went to college; they graduated from Ohio State. I had always told them, "You're gonna grow up, you're gonna go to college and you're going to get off this place." I didn't think it was something that needed discussing. There wasn't enough land to support my two boys and Cedric's three boys.

Jim always understood he was going to leave, but John showed up at home after getting his degree and picked up where he left off. I guess he thought he'd be the one to stay. I told him he had to go, told him, "I don't want you here. You don't have any money and you don't know enough." Maybe that was harsh, but you need a thousand acres of land to farm. The farm had supported two families well for years and we never lacked for anything. But over the past 20 years, things have changed. We still invested as much effort as we ever did, but we didn't get bigger, which is what you have to do to make more. I know they thought it was cold, but we were right to tell the boys to get out on their own.

My oldest son, Jim, has been the county engineer for Darke County for 35 years. We made peace with each other about when he reached his 30's. I never said I was wrong, but somehow my thinking changed and maybe his changed a little, too. My youngest, John, and his wife, Connie, own Premier Feed Company and several other companies. John was even a motivational speaker for a while. I never thought he'd do that.

Isabelle and I had a good marriage. We never had time to have any trouble, didn't have the first argument. Growing up, it seemed like my parents were always fighting about something or other, but we never did. I think the maddest she ever got was once when she thought Ced and I had cut back one of her favorite trees too far. She was fuming and she said, "Those men!"

She was a good person, successful in everything she did. She was a good shot too, quite a marksman. She kept a gun at the backdoor and would shoot groundhogs when they came out from under the chicken house. One afternoon, Jim and his wife Carla were here, and Jim had brought his new rifle. He wanted help getting the sight accurately set. He hadn't hit a tin can yet when Isabelle said, "Let me try." Of course, she hit it on the first shot. Jim told her that must just have been luck, so she took the gun and hit it again. She said, "I don't think it's the gun."

For some reason Isabelle's hair turned gray while she was still in high school. At 75, she got a touch of breast cancer and it must have been the medicine they gave her, but her hair turned dark again-at 75!

When she was 79, the doctor told Isabelle she was as healthy as a 50-year old woman. She was in excellent health at Thanksgiving in 2000 but we buried her the first of February in 2001. The tumor had started in her kidney and grew almost to her heart.

When she died, it was the hardest thing to ever hit me.

My son John jokes that the only vacation I ever had was the war. I guess that's true. In my day, people prided themselves on how much work they could do. I did a lot of work!

I read hundreds of books and still read. I've read all my life whenever I had a spare moment. I was a poor father; I read when I should have been helping with the kids. I read all night long now, from 11:30 at night to 4 in the morning. I don't think anyone ever gets too much knowledge. Isabelle was a reader too, but she was so busy raising chickens, turkeys and kids and taking care of the old folks, she didn't have the time.

Over the years, I've done a lot of talking about the war and a lot of thinking about the war. It was the most important thing I did. I wasn't the buddy kind; I didn't make close friends while I was in the service. There was camaraderie and I got along with everybody but I just wasn't that kind of man. I had the good fortune to see a lot of things other guys didn't get to see, like Paris and Rome. I've often thought since that I should have paid the government for taking me into the army.

The youngest guy of our outfit was the first one to die after the war, from Bell's Palsy. I got the last Christmas card from the only other fellow two years ago, so I guess they're all gone. People like to think country is the reason we fight wars but I've come to believe that wars are fought for one basic reason, and that's money. Back when I was a soldier we looked at war differently then and experienced it differently, too. There were big masses of men. We lost 300 men a day in WWII. Now, no one ever sees the enemy except in very small groups.

My brother Cedric and I grew up together and we grew old together. Not many people have the kind of relationship that we had. We had differences, but not the kind that mattered much. I would buy the least expensive car, he would buy an expensive car, but we both worked hard to get the money for that car. We split everything evenly and we owned everything together, even our homes. We finally did get each house titled in our own name, but that was mostly for the kids' sakes.

If anything seemed like it might cause trouble, I usually just let it go. I didn't like fighting, never wanted to piss anybody off.

I finally retired when I just couldn't work anymore. You slow down. I think when I got beat up by that bull, my body had about all it could take. I think that's maybe that started things downhill. I quit driving in 1998. About three years later, I started sleeping in the lift chair rather than the bed-it was just easier. In the last few years, I've lost the use of my hands and can't walk. The arthritis is pretty bad. I take pain medicine, sometimes all I can get! My right hand closed up and all I can use is my thumbs.

Still, the world doesn't stop just because you're chair-bound. Lot of people stop by to talk, and people call to talk everyday about something. Cedric and I never set out to make any kind of splash, but people around here know us. The Ohio Department of Agriculture has a program that recognizes the contributions made by Ohio's founding farm families and in 2012, our farm was honored as an Ohio Century Farm for being operated by the same family for over 200 years. It seemed fitting to mark that in some way, so that's when I got the big stone out front and had it engraved. Isabelle's family has one too, dated 1847.

At 92, it's harder to get around than it used to be: some parts don't work as well as they should and others don't work at all. I think maybe it's the years of working so hard that took a toll on my hands and legs, but I never minded the work. A man needs to work. Except for the war, I have lived my whole life on the farm. It's where I made my promise to grandpa Lewis and where I kept that promise. This is where I belong, where I have always belonged.

FAREWELL

Maynard Surber died on July 26, 2012. The day before, he'd been short of breath so we took him to the hospital for some tests, thinking a little oxygen or maybe some antibiotics would help. He was his usual practical and irascible self. Frustrated by his inability to produce a urine sample, he said to his grandson, "Oh, hell, Shawn. Just piss in this damn cup and we'll be done!" We brought him home and the next morning, sitting in his worn chair, in the house where he was born, on the farm that defined his character, all life went out of him. An ambulance took him to the hospital, but was already gone. We knew the day would come, but it didn't make losing him any easier.

Maynard was as solid and steady as the rock that stands in front of the Surber homestead. He had an intellectual curiosity and an unending appetite for knowledge that never left him. Although he only left home for as long as it took to serve his country, Maynard embraced his military service as an opportunity to see as much of the world as possible, absorbing every fact, figure and fable along the way.

It was amazing how he remembered everything - dates, times, places, how things happened and why, ten years ago or 500 years ago. He enjoyed an audience, whether he was preaching or just swapping stories with friends and he was as comfortable addressing fifty strangers as he was chatting with the family. There wasn't much he didn't know at least something about, and usually he knew plenty. We weren't the only ones who loved listening to him.

There's such a thing as a good work ethic, and then there's Maynard's work ethic. He thought things should be done a certain way and in a certain time and he wasn't interested in discussing alternatives. Sometimes it even seemed like the job itself wasn't as important as getting it done. He could be inflexible and harsh, but he could be funny too and he and his brother loved to pull a good prank. He was a good man, an honest, hardworking man, who was interested in the world around him and was respected by the many people who knew and depended on him. There are so many ways that we learned from him and so many things that we and our children learned by being with him. He balanced his strong opinions with hard work and his strength of character is the foundation on which our family is built and continues to grow.

It all started with the farm, of course, over 200 years ago. We have made all the legal arrangements to ensure that the land will be part of the Surber family forever but Maynard's life was his real legacy. This book is our way of honoring the man and what he meant -and will always mean- to our family.

Connie and John Surber

It is humbling to summarize the experiences and lessons of nearly sixty years from my father, Maynard Surber.

If I had only one word to describe the man, it would be "responsible." He was forever responsible to his family, his country, his church, and his community. Although there were never enough hours in a day to complete all his planned tasks, he dutifully and abruptly stopped work to attend Army Reserve meetings, lead group singing or perform solo at farm and community events, church revivals and funerals. In later years, he and Isabelle visited all their grandchildren whenever possible and he beamed with pride at their accomplishments.

He was responsible to the Union Church of Christ, serving as chorister, youth teacher, deacon and elder for over fifty years. He adhered steadfastly to a very practical form of religion.

For eighty two years, he honored his childhood commitment to Grandfather Lewis to stay on the family farm, and he left this world in the house where he was born. He was honored by many at his funeral held in the church he had served his entire life, and buried near one corner of the family farm.

He married his high school classmate, Isabelle Donohoo. She was the most important person to him. They had two sons and seven grandchildren and were married over fifty-seven years. I never heard either say an unkind word to, or about, the other. After her death, he echoed terms of endearment anytime he spoke of "Mama" which he did often. Maynard's perseverance after her passing and congeniality over his last eleven years, despite serious physical infirmities, serve as an example to us all.

His stories and accounts of the war were fascinating. He returned from the war a Captain, and much later retired as a Lieutenant Colonel.

After our son Greg visited France, Maynard had many conversations with him, reminiscing over geographic locations where they both had firsthand knowledge. Greg was captivated with his stories and stayed in close contact with him as did all the children. Their love for their Grandpa knew no limits.

Our daughter, Susan, was always coming up with ways to honor him. On his ninetieth birthday, an open house was given with the entire family in attendance. He was ecstatic anytime he had the opportunity to mingle with people.

The latest memories are often the most vivid. Remembering July 22, 2012, Geoff and his wife Jessie sat across from Maynard in his living room. We were discussing world and local events, the arrival of the new great-grandson and a multitude of other topics, as Maynard never lacked for conversation. Brother Cedric arrived with his dog Brandy, Kathy Bright brought in the mail, and the daily parade of people was ongoing. Maynard's presence was felt by everyone, and everyone wanted to share in that presence. Folks came from far and wide to learn from his historical knowledge and to use him as a reference to enhance their family trees.

There are many warm memories of the past shared by all. I am sure my father also had warm memories, along with his steely reality of the present and dreams of the future. Maynard Surber was an optimist, a thinker, a planner, a watcher and a doer. But above all, he was a very responsible man whose commitment to family, community, and country touched more people than most can hope for in a lifetime. He will forever be cherished and missed by all of us.

Jim and Carla Surber

Memories of Pappaw

Shawn:

When I was about 5-6 years old, I went to their house over the weekend and went to the milkhouse for the Sunday evening milking. There was Pappaw and Uncle Ceddy milking cows. They were both sitting on stools with hats on, their heads pressed against the side of the cow causing tons of cow hair to be on both of their hats. About that time a cow kicked and cow poop flew through the air and covered my face. I'm sure the look on my face was priceless. Pappaw and Uncle Ceddy both looked over and saw the poop all over me and busted out laughing – as only they could together. They were also covered in poop and had tobacco juice running down their face. I just remember them laughing.

I remember one time I was at Pappaw's and the walnut trees needed spraying. The entire batch of Roundup was mixed up and put into milk jugs to transport it to the field. Before we left, we had a full belly from Mammaw. Each time we'd climb into the truck, Pappaw reminded me to wipe my feet before I got in despite the truck being covered in mud, poop, and tobacco. Then, Pappaw drove in reverse all the way to Surber road, rather than just turning around and driving down in forward. Then we went to the milk house and filled the milk cans with water and Roundup without measuring anything and went to Donohoo's to do the job. Pappaw stood there and pointed with his cane telling me to not worry about how I sprayed – just spray! By the time I finished the first row, Pappaw was able to calculate how much water in total we would need, how much Round up, how many minutes it should take to finish the job, and if we needed to go back to the barn to get more water. Pappaw was never concerned about how something got done, just that it got done. I asked several times how exactly he wanted the job to be done, but he'd just respond, "It don't matter – just do it! Spray it in a circle; just spray!"

Mammaw always let you pick the kind of cake or icing for your birthday, which made you feel special and important. My favorite meal was our Sunday dinner and anytime she made her baked steak, gravy, mashed potatoes and noodles. She would have cooked anything that we wanted, and would ask for requests since she often said she felt like she cooked the same thing over and over.

Shawn Surber, 36, son of John and Connie

Shannon:

Mammaw and Pappaw were both unique - and fantastic. Mammaw always hugged me goodbye and told me I was precious. She was one of the most generous people I've ever known. She was always making something for someone else. She was a fabulous cook and always cooked things she knew we would love, like homemade noodles and corn, cinnamon rolls from leftover pie crust, and caramel-icing flower cookies with sprinkles, just to name a few.

She had beautiful penmanship and hand-wrote all her letters. She wrote a letter to someone every day and wrote to her sister once a week, so she loved going to the mailbox. She knew she would have letters in return. I always anticipated letters from her when I was away at college. I remember how she laughed a lot, how she enjoyed rocking in her chair, and that she was a whiz at crossword puzzles.

When I think of Pappaw, I think "big". He was big himself, and he had a big voice, big hands, a big laugh and big personality.

When we walked through the front door, he always asked,"What's this outfit?"

His depth of knowledge on a variety of topics was such that he could carry on a conversation with just about anyone about just about anything and had no problem expressing his opinion.

His truck was always a mess. He thought it was hilarious to ask you to wipe your feet before you got in it and then laugh and laugh.

He was proud to be a member of the community, proud to be a farmer, and proud to be a Surber. I miss them.

Shannon Surber, 35, daughter of John and Connie

Geoff:

From the time I was less than 2 years old, I spent a lot of my childhood with Grandpa and Grandma Surber. Those were probably some of the happiest times of my life. When I was ten years old or so, he would tell me of his experiences in the war and the towns and people in Europe.

From my earliest recollection, I always looked at Grandpa and considered him "impending doom." While he certainly never was mean or unkind to me, he always projected a no-nonsense image that is never popular with a young boy. But as I grew older, Grandpa and I became close friends, especially after Grandma died. We talked on the phone every few days all the time I was in college. After graduation, he became very interested in my business and real estate investments and we talked at length about them. He would listen and ask questions, but never tell me what he thought I should do. I appreciated that.

He was very happy when Jessie and I got married and he thought she was the perfect wife for me. Grandpa told Jessie that the perfect way to handle me was to treat me like a donkey and hit me in the head with a 2x4 when I needed it.

On July 12, 2012, two weeks before he died, I spoke with Grandpa and made notes while I talked with him. He knew Jessie and I were expecting a baby in December and I told him we were having a hard time coming up with a name we liked. He talked about how having a unique name was an advantage. He said Maynard and Cedric were uncommon names and I believe he said that his mom liked the names but his dad didn't. He talked about what a disadvantage having kid-like names could be. He said it would be difficult for anyone to take a 50- year old man named "Ricky" seriously.

He went on to give me all the male and female family names in the Surber family. I had heard his stories about his own grandfather Lewis before, but can't remember him giving much detail about any of the others. I later called him back and told him "Lewis" sounded the best and

Jessie agreed. I told him we had a winner. He seemed very happy with it and we are too.

Grandpa always appeared to be concerned with family above all else. His life, after Grandma's passing and for the next eleven years, seemed to center around the family and his interest in what they were doing.

Geoff Surber, 33, son of Jim and Carla

Traci:

One weekend, the other kids and I stayed the night at Mammaw and Pappaw's house. Mammaw had cooked homemade noodles, one of my favorite dishes. I helped her in the kitchen, eating more than I was actually helping. Then we all sat together and ate the meal, which we always did. After eating, I laid on the register, which caused the noodles-raw and cooked-to swell in my stomach. I remember laying on the register complaining "I'm gonna die!!!" I also wanted Mom and Dad! Pappaw just laughed and pointed out that I would just be just fine, I wasn't going to die and I didn't need my mom and dad.

I also remember each time that you were sitting on a chair with your feet up, as Pappaw would walk by, he'd grab your big toe and say, "wee, wee, wee!" in a high pitched voice.

Traci Surber, 31, daughter of John and Connie

Susan:

When I think of my grandpa from the first moments I can remember the words that come to mind to describe him are "undeniably principled." He lived his life righteously – a hard-working, church-going, law-abiding, former military man making a living on a three-generation, family-operated farm. Whereas my grandmother would dote upon us and we could rarely do wrong in her eyes, my grandfather wanted to instill his sense of virtue into his grandchildren.

When my brothers and I would visit my grandparents for an extended stay, my grandma wanted us to enjoy ourselves ceaselessly. She always cooked our favorite meals regardless of how many meals in a row we requested hamburger gravy. She always bought new kites for us to fly in the cow pastures, and I was always greeted with several new outfits, hand sewn just for me. We got to sleep in until the late hours of the morning.

Vacation with them was wonderful. Sometimes we would sleep a little too late and my grandma would come in to wake us up saying we had better get up before Grandpa saw us still in bed. Grandma would only allow us a small breakfast when we would sleep late because she thought it might ruin our appetite for lunchtime and then grandpa would know we had slept in too late. When he would come in for lunch (also known as dinner on the farm), sometimes he would catch us still in our pajamas with sleepy eyes and ask if we had just woken up. We would guiltily respond "yes" and he always said the same thing, "You will get bed sores from sleeping so much!" Then we would sit down for dinner and be eating hamburger gravy for the fourth dinner in a row. He would say, "Hamburger gravy again, can't these kids eat anything else?" then dutifully eat the meal prepared for him saying nothing else.

As we grew up, we were given more responsibilities – emptying the "slop bucket" (leftovers for composting – not even fit for the barn cats to eat), baling hay, hoeing the weeds in the garden, watering the flowers, and cleaning the house. One summer, my brothers and I were expected to repaint the fence row lining the east side of the house. We painted much of the fence, but got distracted when we started to paint each other. My older brother warned that, "Grandpa is going to beat our butts if don't finish this job." My younger brother and I proceeded to play in the paint. And my older brother's warnings were accurate; we were quite fearful of what our grandfather would do to us when he saw there was probably more paint on the three of us than on the fence row.

I don't ever remember grandpa physically punishing us for our indiscretions, but we always knew how he felt. He expected more from us and that is how I remember him with others. His expectation for his family and community to live righteously is his most important legacy.

But my grandfather was not always so austere. My most memorable time spent with him was sitting on his lap reading bedtime stories. I would pick my book for the night and climb onto his lap as he sat in his recliner. He had a distinct smell of chewing tobacco - which he kept in the breast pockets of his shirt - and Barbasol shaving cream that I can still smell as if it were yesterday. We generally read my favorite book from their collection, *The Gull That Lost the Sea*. He would read to me and I would practice my reading to him. We sometimes sat together after reading and discussed the important happenings of my life. I would giggle when he tickled me and we enjoyed each other's company until bedtime. It was our savored moment at the end of the day.

Susan (Surber) Wojcicki, 29, daughter of James and Carla

Greg:

One of my most vivid memories of Grandpa comes from my childhood. It was a Sunday morning at the Union Church of Christ. I believe I was 10 years old, which meant I was expected to join the other children for Sunday School while the adults had a separate service. I loved the opening service, as it was a chance to sing. Grandpa led the congregation in the hymns, and up to that point, it was the only role I knew he had in the church. When the opening service was ending, I asked if I could stay with Grandma and the family for the main service. While I enjoyed Sunday School, I was curious about what took place when the children left.

After introductory remark bys the pastor, Grandpa rose and faced the crowd behind the podium. This was my first surprise. While I knew he was active in the church, this was the first occasion I witnessed any non-clergyman give a lesson in church. I had spent so much time with Grandpa, but I had not known him to be a public speaker. I was proud of him and my family in that moment, that he was so respected in the community to be given this responsibility.

This surprise was not what affected me, however. Instead, it was the lesson Grandpa shared. Even by that age, I had grown accustomed to the rhetoric of clergymen. It was a style that emphasized inclusion and community, voices that spoke of the sacrifice and love of Christ with a firm but soothing tone. Grandpa's own lesson spoke of these ideas, but it was different. He spoke with passion, but his style was much more immediate and matter-of-fact, shorn of the practiced rhetoric of the preachers I had heard before.

Grandpa's lesson was filled with historical allusions and names I could identify: Napoleon, Hitler, current world leaders. He wove in these stories to illustrate the corruption of power, the folly of arrogance, and the dangers of forgetting the lessons of history. While I was too young to understand these references completely, his lesson hit me in a way that others had not before. Grandpa was sharing parables from the past to teach the Word of Christ. I cannot remember the passage or the verses that served as the foundation of the lesson. I'm not sure I knew even then. But it didn't matter. Each Sunday I spent at Union thereafter, I stayed with the main congregation to participate in the service.

As I grew older and learned more about the world, I had the opportunity to hear of Grandpa's experiences in life - as a child, in the war, on the farm - and understand his lessons in a different setting. Those lessons were passed down not only to me but to the whole community of which Maynard was a part. It is no surprise that so many people visited him often to hear his thoughts and recollections, which he was more than happy to share. And as I think back on all the things I have pursued in my life - music, history, public speaking - perhaps I did not discover my love for them on my own, but instead I am carrying forward just some of the passions Grandpa shared with all of us.

Greg Surber, 27, son of Jim and Carla

Todd:

My favorite memory from Mammaw and Pappaw's farm was shearing day for the angora goats. They ran the goats into the barn lot and through the old milking parlor, one at a time. Mammaw instructed me on my duties, as I was small enough to watch from under the table where they kept their tools. First, they sheared the goats, rolling them in different directions to achieve a smooth stretch for the shears. It was my job to collect the mohair and stuff it into a sack under the table. I watched Mammaw and Pappaw trim hooves, dip the goats in a bath, and de-worm them with a liquid. Then the animal was released and it was my responsibility to place a kernel of corn in a can to keep count of the number of head we had sheared for the day.

Among my favorite memories were the Sunday dinners we enjoyed at the Surber Farm. When arriving, with the first step into the house, each of us got our own unique greeting from Pappaw and he'd ask, "What kind of outfit is this?!" He always inspired a smile. Some of us would assist Mammaw in the kitchen and the rest visited in the living room until dinner was ready. The menu was consistent, always better each time than I remembered. Mammaw teased us on occasion about having ham sandwiches but she knew how much we enjoyed her "usual" dinner. In fact, I'd have been disappointed if we'd had anything else. The "usual" was baked steak cooked on an iron skillet and finished off in the oven. From that, she made an amazing gravy with mashed potatoes (my favorite), sweet corn that she had planted, harvested, picked, shucked, silked, cooked, bagged, frozen, thawed then prepared herself, homemade rolls with butter (cousin Greg always favored "a little roll with his butter"), plus cookies and pie. Pappaw said grace, then we passed dishes clockwise around the table until everyone had a full plate. I remember times when we were interrupted by a cry from a "kid", an angora goat with its head stuck in the fence beside Pappaw's house. He said, "When raising animals, one must always be close. Even if you're just rocking on the front porch, it'll pay off." After dinner, conversation resumed in the living room. Pappaw would settle back in his chair, pull some tobacco from his shirt pocket and bite off a piece with the side of his mouth.

I remember we kids thought there was buried treasure under the front porch and I remember putting up hay the old way with Uncle Ceddy. Ceddy would have tobacco juice running down the wrinkles on the sides of his mouth, staining the white tee shirt under his blue work shirt. He would drive the tractor and park his cane on a handle bar next to the steering wheel. At the end of the day, when the work was done, we'd stop for a drink from the well by the milk house and have ham sandwiches, pop, and a cookie under the shade of trees. The experience inspired me to write a song, *Puttin' Up Hay the Old Way.* I still sing it and remember.

Todd Surber, 29, son of John and Connie

Brooklin:

I remember playing with the old, iron, child's kitchen playset that was on the landing of the stairs at Pappaw's. I would take M&Ms and put them into the cups and bowls and 'serve' the family tea. Everyone would sit in the living room and I would go around and give each person their tea, take their empty dishware, and fill it up again in the "kitchen" which was on the landing of the stairs.

Pappaw would always say grace at the beginning of a meal. When I was about three, I asked if I could say grace before the meal. Pappaw gave permission and so I said the grace for that meal. Until his death, afterwards Pappaw always let me say grace before the meal.

Brooklin, 12, first great-grandchild,
daughter of Shawn and Rebecca

Photo Album

Four generations. L-R: Earl Surber (father), John Perry (great grandfather), Maynard (as a baby), Lewis (grandfather)

Grandfather Lewis, at the reins, with friend

Cedric and Maynard

Maynard and Cedric

Maynard (wearing hat) and Cedric tending their hogs

Maynard with a Guernsey at Ohio State University

Maynard, High School graduation

Isabelle, High School Graduation

Maynard, young entrepreneur

Isabelle, on the job with Farm Services

Maynard and Isabelle, sweethearts

Isabelle and Maynard on their wedding day

Isabelle with Maynard, in his cavalry boots, before shipping off to Europe

Isabelle sends greetings from the farm to Maynard in Europe

Hired hands with Earl, 2nd from left, and Cedric, hand on dog, and haystack tarped and held down by cans filled with rocks

To Mr/Mrs EARL L. SURBER
Hillsboro #1
OHIO
USA June 12/44

(CENSOR'S STAMP)

V—MAIL

Dear Folks,

[handwritten V-mail letter, signed] Love, Maynard

V-mail to the folks

Lt. Maynard Surber and members of his unit

Fort DuBambois Interior

Building a pontoon bridge

Safe crossing over a pontoon bridge

Using the crane to build a pontoon bridge

Bridge across the Rhine

A Bailey bridge in France

Tank destroyers crossing a Bailey bridge

The Surber farm

A typical Ayrshire on the Surber farm, machinery shed in back

Ganelle and Earl on their 50th anniversary

Maynard leading the singing at Union Church

Maynard and Isabelle, annual church picture

Maynard and Isabelle's 50th anniversary-Back row:Shawn, Carla, Isabelle, Connie.
Second row: Geoff, Jim, Susan, Shannon (in white), Greg, Maynard, John, Traci.
Seated on floor: Todd

Another four generations, John, Maynard, Shawn, Brooklin, 2007

Connie and John Surber

The Union Church of Christ

The Surber Family Home, summer 2013

In 1994, a detailed collection of family history, family records and genealogy of the Surber family was compiled by James Surber. Copies of the document are readily available from the family for viewing or research.

Scrapbooks of many of Maynard's service records, early family photographs, additional farm photographs, wedding invitations and materials too delicate or difficult to reproduce have been preserved and are in the care of Connie and John Surber.

Maynard's original recordings about his military service, the history of the Union Church and the early Surber family history have been carefully copied and distributed to family members who are at liberty to share them as they wish.

From Mammaw's Kitchen

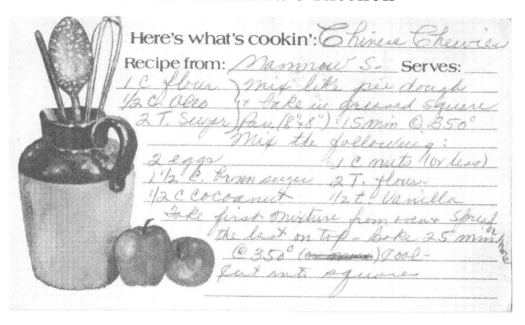

Here's what's cookin': *Chinese Chewies*

Recipe from: *Mammaw's* Serves: ___

1 C flour) mix like pie dough
½ C oleo) & bake in greased square
2 T. sugar) pan (8"x8") 15 min @ 350°
Mix the following:
2 eggs   1 C nuts (or less)
1½ C. brown sugar   2 T. flour
½ C coconut   ½ t. Vanilla
Take first mixture from oven spread
the last on top - Bake 25 min
@ 350° (   ) Cool -
Cut into squares

Isabelle's handwritten, most-requested recipe for Chinese Chewies

Pimento Spread or add to cheese + Pickle + Mayonaise for Cheese Salad

1½ doz Pimentos (Red) ground fine
1 C sugar
1 C Vinegar
1 t. salt
1 t. ground mustard
Cook until tender then add 3 T. flour
to thicken. Put in Small jars & freeze

Isabelle's favorite for social gatherings, Pimento Cheese Sandwiches

The Ancestors of Maynard Surber
04/14/1920 – 07/26/2012

Earl Lester Surber 12/19/1892 - 02/27/1964
and Ganelle Ruth Roberts 05/12/1893 – 04/03/1976

Lewis Allen Surber 02/02/1868 - 05/05/1930
and Anna Pegan 10/24/1869 – 01/28/1955

John Perry Surber 08/10/1832 - 05/05/1924
and Jennie Mariah Davidson 02/25/1840 – 04/24/1917

Henry Surber (Jr.) 12/25/1799 - 10/16/1866
and Catherine Fender 05/23/1801   03/02/1883

Henry Surber   b. 1775 - 10/01/1857
and Catherine Coffman   d. 05/12/1801

Jacob Surber   b. 1744 - 08/23/1839
and Catherine Haller Coffeld 1742 – 1820

Hans Heinrich Surber   01/08/1719 d. 1795

Heinrich Surber   03/20/1683 – 09/28/1754
and Barbara Schmidt   d. 1731

Jacob Surber   10/08/1655 - d. 1682

Hans Surber   b. 06/06/1624

Michael Surber b. 1582 d. 1643

Puttin' Up Hay the Old Way
song by: Todd Surber

'Puttin up hay the old way,
Gonna circle round a field on a Monday afternoon,
Hang on boys, were gonna get done real soon
Take a swaller of some water in the heat of the sun
Pick up the bales do it one by one
Stack em on the wagon do it left to right
Long in the middle and try to keep it tight
Pull it with the tractor and take it to the barn
Toss it in the mow till we need it for the farm
Hang on boys were putting up hay the old way
Don't take the sweat out of farming
It'll do you right
It will wake u up In the morning and put u to bed at night
It's what makes the old mare go
Gonna do it all again when the rooster crows
Hang on boys were putting up hay the old way'

Made in the USA
Lexington, KY
23 July 2014